THE RESPIRATORY SYSTEM

THE ENCYCLOPEDIA OF
HEALTH

THE HEALTHY BODY

Dale C. Garell, M.D. · General Editor

THE RESPIRATORY SYSTEM

Mary Kittredge

Introduction by C. Everett Koop, M.D., Sc.D.
Surgeon General, U.S. Public Health Service

CHELSEA HOUSE PUBLISHERS
New York Philadelphia

The goal of the ENCYCLOPEDIA OF HEALTH *is to provide general information in the ever-changing areas of physiology, psychology, and related medical issues. The titles in this series are not intended to take the place of the professional advice of a physician or other health-care professional.*

ON THE COVER: Computer generated image of human lungs

Chelsea House Publishers
EDITOR-IN-CHIEF: Nancy Toff
EXECUTIVE EDITOR: Remmel T. Nunn
MANAGING EDITOR: Karyn Gullen Browne
COPY CHIEF: Juliann Barbato
PICTURE EDITOR: Adrian G. Allen
ART DIRECTOR: Maria Epes
MANUFACTURING MANAGER: Gerald Levine

The Encyclopedia of Health
SENIOR EDITOR: Jane Larkin Crain

Staff for THE RESPIRATORY SYSTEM
ASSISTANT EDITOR: Laura Dolce
DEPUTY COPY CHIEF: Ellen Scordato
EDITORIAL ASSISTANT: Jennifer Trachtenberg
PICTURE RESEARCHER: Debra J. Hershkowitz
DESIGN: Debbie Jay, Jean Weis
DESIGNER: Marie-Hélène Fredericks
ASSISTANT DESIGNER: Marjorie Zaum
PRODUCTION COORDINATOR: Joseph Romano

First Printing

1 3 5 7 9 8 6 4 2

Library of Congress Cataloging-in-Publication Data
Kittredge, Mary, 1949–
The Respiratory system / Mary Kittredge.
p. cm.—(The Encyclopedia of health)
Bibliography p.
Includes index.
ISBN 0-7910-0026-5
0-7910-0467-8 (pbk.)
1. Respiration—Juvenile literature. I. Title. II. Series.
QP121.K64 1988 88-4069
612'.2—dc 19 CIP

CONTENTS

THE ENCYCLOPEDIA OF
HEALTH

THE HEALTHY BODY

The Circulatory System
Dental Health
The Digestive System
The Endocrine System
Exercise
Genetics & Heredity
The Human Body: An Overview
Hygiene
The Immune System
Memory & Learning
The Musculoskeletal System
The Neurological System
Nutrition
The Reproductive System
The Respiratory System
The Senses
Speech & Hearing
Sports Medicine
Vision
Vitamins & Minerals

THE LIFE CYCLE

Adolescence
Adulthood
Aging
Childhood
Death & Dying
The Family
Friendship & Love
Pregnancy & Birth

MEDICAL ISSUES

Careers in Health Care
Environmental Health
Folk Medicine
Health Care Delivery
Holistic Medicine
Medical Ethics
Medical Fakes & Frauds
Medical Technology
Medicine & the Law
Occupational Health
Public Health

PSYCHOLOGICAL DISORDERS AND THEIR TREATMENT

Anxiety & Phobias
Child Abuse
Compulsive Behavior
Delinquency & Criminal Behavior
Depression
Diagnosing & Treating Mental Illness
Eating Habits & Disorders
Learning Disabilities
Mental Retardation
Personality Disorders
Schizophrenia
Stress Management
Suicide

MEDICAL DISORDERS AND THEIR TREATMENT

AIDS
Allergies
Alzheimer's Disease
Arthritis
Birth Defects
Cancer
The Common Cold
Diabetes
Drugs: Prescription & OTC
First Aid & Emergency Medicine
Gynecological Disorders
Headaches
The Hospital
Kidney Disorders
Medical Diagnosis
The Mind-Body Connection
Mononucleosis & Other Infectious Diseases
Nuclear Medicine
Organ Transplants
Pain
Physical Handicaps
Poisons & Toxins
Sexually Transmitted Diseases
Skin Diseases
Stroke & Heart Disease
Substance Abuse
Tropical Medicine

PREVENTION AND EDUCATION: THE KEYS TO GOOD HEALTH

C. Everett Koop, M.D., Sc.D.
Surgeon General,
U.S. Public Health Service

The issue of health education has received particular attention in recent years because of the presence of AIDS in the news. But our response to this particular tragedy points up a number of broader issues that doctors, public health officials, educators, and the public face. In particular, it points up the necessity for sound health education for citizens of all ages.

Over the past 25 years this country has been able to bring about dramatic declines in the death rates for heart disease, stroke, accidents, and, for people under the age of 45, cancer. Today, Americans generally eat better and take better care of themselves than ever before. Thus, with the help of modern science and technology, they have a better chance of surviving serious—even catastrophic—illnesses. That's the good news.

But, like every phonograph record, there's a flip side, and one with special significance for young adults. According to a report issued in 1979 by Dr. Julius Richmond, my predecessor as Surgeon General, Americans aged 15 to 24 had a higher death rate in 1979 than they did 20 years earlier. The causes: violent death and injury, alcohol and drug abuse, unwanted pregnancies, and sexually transmitted diseases. Adolescents are particularly vulnerable, because they are beginning to explore their own sexuality and perhaps to experiment with drugs. The need for educating young people is critical, and the price of neglect is high.

Yet even for the population as a whole, our health is still far from what it could be. Why? A 1974 Canadian government report attributed all death and disease to four broad elements: inadequacies in the health-care system, behavioral factors or unhealthy life-styles, environmental hazards, and human biological factors.

To be sure, there are diseases that are still beyond the control of even our advanced medical knowledge and techniques. And despite yearnings that are as old as the human race itself, there is no "fountain of youth" to ward off aging and death. Still, there is a solution to many of the problems that undermine sound health. In a word, that solution is prevention. Prevention, which includes health promotion and education, saves lives, improves the quality of life, and, in the long run, saves money.

In the United States, organized public health activities and preventive medicine have a long history. Important milestones include the improvement of sanitary procedures and the development of pasteurized milk in the late 19th century, and the introduction in the mid-20th century of effective vaccines against polio, measles, German measles, mumps, and other once-rampant diseases. Internationally, organized public health efforts began on a wide-scale basis with the International Sanitary Conference of 1851, to which 12 nations sent representatives. The World Health Organization, founded in 1948, continues these efforts under the aegis of the United Nations, with particular emphasis on combatting communicable diseases and the training of health-care workers.

But despite these accomplishments, much remains to be done in the field of prevention. For too long, we have had a medical care system that is science- and technology-based, focused, essentially, on illness and mortality. It is now patently obvious that both the social and the economic costs of such a system are becoming insupportable.

Implementing prevention—and its corollaries, health education and promotion—is the job of several groups of people:

First, the medical and scientific professions need to continue basic scientific research, and here we are making considerable progress. But increased concern with prevention will also have a decided impact on how primary-care doctors practice medicine. With a shift to health-based rather than morbidity-based medicine, the role of the "new physician" will include a healthy dose of patient education.

Second, practitioners of the social and behavioral sciences—psychologists, economists, city planners—along with lawyers, business leaders, and government officials—must solve the practical and ethical dilemmas confronting us: poverty, crime, civil rights, literacy, education, employment, housing, sanitation, environmental protection, health care delivery systems, and so forth. All of these issues affect public health.

Third is the public at large. We'll consider that very important group in a moment.

Fourth, and the linchpin in this effort, is the public health profession—doctors, epidemiologists, teachers—who must harness the professional expertise of the first two groups and the common sense and cooperation of the third, the public. They must define the problems statistically and qualitatively and then help us set priorities for finding the solutions.

To a very large extent, improving those statistics is the responsibility of every individual. So let's consider more specifically what the role of the individual should be and why health education is so important to that role. First, and most obviously, individuals can protect themselves from illness and injury and thus minimize their need for professional medical care. They can eat a nutritious diet, get adequate exercise, avoid tobacco, alcohol, and drugs, and take prudent steps to avoid accidents. The proverbial "apple a day keeps the doctor away" is not so far from the truth, after all.

Second, individuals should actively participate in their own medical care. They should schedule regular medical and dental checkups. Should they develop an illness or injury, they should know when to treat themselves and when to seek professional help. To gain the maximum benefit from any medical treatment that they do require, individuals must become partners in that treatment. For instance, they should understand the effects and side effects of medications. I counsel young physicians that there is no such thing as too much information when talking with patients. But the corollary is the patient must know enough about the nuts and bolts of the healing process to understand what the doctor is telling him. That is at least partially the patient's responsibility.

Education is equally necessary for us to understand the ethical and public policy issues in health care today. Sometimes individuals will encounter these issues in making decisions about their own treatment or that of family members. Other citizens may encounter them as jurors in medical malpractice cases. But we all become involved, indirectly, when we elect our public officials, from school board members to the president. Should surrogate parenting be legal? To what extent is drug testing desirable, legal, or necessary? Should there be public funding for family planning, hospitals, various types of medical research, and medical care for the indigent? How should we allocate scant technological resources, such as kidney dialysis and organ transplants? What is the proper role of government in protecting the rights of patients?

What are the broad goals of public health in the United States today? In 1980, the Public Health Service issued a report aptly entitled *Promoting Health-Preventing Disease: Objectives for the Nation.* This report expressed its goals in terms of mortality and in terms of intermediate goals in education and health improvement. It identified 15 major concerns: controlling high blood pressure; improving family planning; improving pregnancy care and infant health; increasing the rate of immunization; controlling sexually transmitted diseases; controlling the presence of toxic agents and radiation in the environment; improving occupational safety and health; preventing accidents; promoting water fluoridation and dental health; controlling infectious diseases; decreasing smoking; decreasing alcohol and drug abuse; improving nutrition; promoting physical fitness and exercise; and controlling stress and violent behavior.

For healthy adolescents and young adults (ages 15 to 24), the specific goal was a 20% reduction in deaths, with a special focus on motor vehicle injuries and alcohol and drug abuse. For adults (ages 25 to 64), the aim was 25% fewer deaths, with a concentration on heart attacks, strokes, and cancers.

Smoking is perhaps the best example of how individual behavior can have a direct impact on health. Today cigarette smoking is recognized as the most important single preventable cause of death in our society. It is responsible for more cancers and more cancer deaths than any other known agent; is a prime risk factor for heart and blood vessel disease, chronic bronchitis, and emphysema; and is a frequent cause of complications in pregnancies and of babies born prematurely, underweight, or with potentially fatal respiratory and cardiovascular problems.

Since the release of the Surgeon General's first report on smoking in 1964, the proportion of adult smokers has declined substantially, from 43% in 1965 to 30.5% in 1985. Since 1965, 37 million people have quit smoking. Although there is still much work to be done if we are to become a "smoke-free society," it is heartening to note that public health and public education efforts—such as warnings on cigarette packages and bans on broadcast advertising—have already had significant effects.

In 1835, Alexis de Tocqueville, a French visitor to America, wrote, "In America the passion for physical well-being is general." Today, as then, health and fitness are front-page items. But with the greater scientific and technological resources now available to us, we are in a far stronger position to make good health care available to everyone. And with the greater technological threats to us as we approach the 21st century, the need to do so is more urgent than ever before. Comprehensive information about basic biology, preventive medicine, medical and surgical treatments, and related ethical and public policy issues can help you arm yourself with the knowledge you need to be healthy throughout your life.

FOREWORD

Dale C. Garell, M.D.

Advances in our understanding of health and disease during the 20th century have been truly remarkable. Indeed, it could be argued that modern health care is one of the greatest accomplishments in all of human history. In the early 1900s, improvements in sanitation, water treatment, and sewage disposal reduced death rates and increased longevity. Previously untreatable illnesses can now be managed with antibiotics, immunizations, and modern surgical techniques. Discoveries in the fields of immunology, genetic diagnosis, and organ transplantation are revolutionizing the prevention and treatment of disease. Modern medicine is even making inroads against cancer and heart disease, two of the leading causes of death in the United States.

Although there is much to be proud of, medicine continues to face enormous challenges. Science has vanquished diseases such as smallpox and polio, but new killers, most notably AIDS, confront us. Moreover, we now victimize ourselves with what some have called "diseases of choice," or those brought on by drug and alcohol abuse, bad eating habits, and mismanagement of the stresses and strains of contemporary life. The very technology that is doing so much to prolong life has brought with it previously unimaginable ethical dilemmas related to issues of death and dying. The rising cost of health-care is a matter of central concern to us all. And violence in the form of automobile accidents, homicide, and suicide remain the major killers of young adults.

In the past, most people were content to leave health care and medical treatment in the hands of professionals. But since the 1960s, the consumer of medical care—that is, the patient—has assumed an increasingly central role in the management of his or her own health. There has also been a new emphasis placed on prevention: People are recognizing that their own actions can help prevent many of the conditions that have caused death and disease in the past. This accounts for the growing commitment to good nutrition and regular exercise, for the fact that more and more people are choosing not to smoke, and for a new moderation in people's drinking habits.

People want to know more about themselves and their own health. They are curious about their body: its anatomy, physiology, and biochemistry. They want to keep up with rapidly evolving medical technologies and procedures. They are willing to educate themselves about common disorders and diseases so that they can be full partners in their own health-care.

The ENCYCLOPEDIA OF HEALTH is designed to provide the basic knowledge that readers will need if they are to take significant responsibility for their own health. It is also meant to serve as a frame of reference for further study and exploration. The ENCYCLOPEDIA is divided into five subsections: The Healthy Body; The Life Cycle; Medical Disorders & Their Treatment; Psychological Disorders & Their Treatment; and Medical Issues. For each topic covered by the ENCYCLOPEDIA, we present the essential facts about the relevant biology; the symptoms, diagnosis, and treatment of common diseases and disorders; and ways in which you can prevent or reduce the severity of health problems when that is possible. The ENCYCLOPEDIA also projects what may lie ahead in the way of future treatment or prevention strategies.

The broad range of topics and issues covered in the ENCYCLOPEDIA reflects the fact that human health encompasses physical, psychological, social, environmental, and spiritual well-being. Just as the mind and the body are inextricably linked, so, too, is the individual an integral part of the wider world that comprises his or her family, society, and environment. To discuss health in its broadest aspect it is necessary to explore the many ways in which it is connected to such fields as law, social science, public policy, economics, and even religion. And so, the ENCYCLOPEDIA is meant to be a bridge between science, medical technology, the world at large, and you. I hope that it will inspire you to pursue in greater depth particular areas of interest, and that you will take advantage of the suggestions for further reading and the lists of resources and organizations that can provide additional information.

AUTHOR'S PREFACE

THE RESPIRATORY SYSTEM

Imagine a large factory that performs many tasks and produces many different products. At the core of this factory is a delicate, complex system of machinery. Running day and night, 7 days a week, year in and year out, the system's largest moving parts cycle at the rate of 720 times per hour and 17,280 times a day. Its smallest parts, some too small to be seen with the naked eye, work even faster and just as steadily.

Over its lifetime, which may be as long as 100 years or so, this system will perform its essential task an astonishing 650 million times. Yet it rarely malfunctions or even needs a tune-up; in fact, in addition to its regular work, it automatically does almost all of its own maintenance, cleanup, and repair.

This is fortunate, for the system's parts are nearly all hidden and difficult to reach. Not only that, but on the rare occasions when the system does break down, disaster quickly ensues. Within three minutes of such a breakdown, both the system and the entire factory fall into total and irreparable ruin, never to run again.

Such a wondrous and essential system may seem to be the stuff of science fiction, not fact. But in reality, each human being possesses one of these remarkable systems in his or her own body. It is the respiratory system: the complex and marvelous machinery by which the human body—the "factory"—supplies itself with air.

Along with food and water, air is one of the three great necessities for life. But although a person may survive many days without food, and for a few days without water—because supplies of these are stored in the body's tissues—the human body must constantly take in fresh air, for its stores of this necessity will sustain it for only about three minutes. After that, it begins to die. This is why we do not get hungry or thirsty for several hours after eating or drinking but become quite uncomfortable after holding our breath for just a few moments. The discomfort is the body's way of demanding more air.

Because the body's need to take in air is so immediate and essential, it has developed a complex, efficient, and almost foolproof system for doing so. Parts of the respiratory system warm the air to the temperature of the body and filter it to remove bits of injurious foreign matter. Other parts perform "housekeeping" and self-repair chores, constantly removing particles that have managed to get by earlier defenses and hunting for and destroying invaders such as bacteria in the lung tissues. Some parts of the respiratory system even build blockades to prevent certain diseases, such as tuberculosis, from spreading.

Still other parts of the respiratory system channel air down into the lungs, where in tiny chambers called *alveoli,* molecules of oxygen—the element in air that is essential to life—pass through thin tissue membranes into the blood. The blood carries oxygen to all of the body's cells, which use it in their constant, necessary task of metabolism: turning food into energy.

But breathing is not only a process of taking in fresh air. The old saying, "In with the good, out with the bad," accurately describes the two essential parts of every breath: *inhalation* (breathing in) and *exhalation* (breathing out).

Just as oxygen passes into the blood through the alveoli, so carbon dioxide—a waste product of metabolism—passes out from the blood into the alveoli and is expelled from the body when we exhale. Without this cleansing function of the respiratory system, the human body would be poisoned by its own waste products as surely as it would suffocate without oxygen—although not quite as quickly.

Thus we depend on the respiratory system to sustain our very existence from moment to moment, yet most of the time it works so well that we do not even notice its functioning. We breathe without thinking about it, 12 times a minute, waking and sleeping, day in and day out for our entire lives.

Smoke pours from the chimney of a steel mill. Industrial pollution poses a serious threat to the respiratory system.

But there are threats to this wonderful and ingenious system. Chief among them is cigarette smoking, a lung-destroying addiction that causes more than 300,000 deaths every year. Other dangers to the respiratory system are asthma, cystic fibrosis, congenital (from birth) defects, and infectious (caused by germs) pneumonia. Drug and alcohol overdoses are another two causes of respiratory failure to which both young people and adults are susceptible. Finally, air pollution—in the home, in public, and in the workplace—represents a huge and subtle threat to the respiratory systems both of young people living today and to the children they may someday want to raise.

Medicine, stop-smoking programs, clean-air laws, and public-health measures can do a great deal to safeguard the respiratory system from these threats. In addition, research is constantly under way to find new methods of preventing and curing lung diseases. But the best defense for the respiratory system of a young person—and any person—is knowledge.

This volume is designed to help young people and all who care about them to learn more about the respiratory system: what it is, how it works, and how to take care of it. In it, they will learn what ancient peoples believed about air and breathing and how modern knowledge on these topics was acquired. They will discover how and why all living things breathe, as well as the many different parts of the human respiratory system and how they work.

The volume discusses what can go wrong with the respiratory system and what can be done to prevent and treat breathing problems. It explains how to recognize and cope with breathing emergencies and how to get more information about the respiratory system from agencies and associations devoted to protecting and defending the "breath of life."

CHAPTER 1

THE BREATH OF LIFE

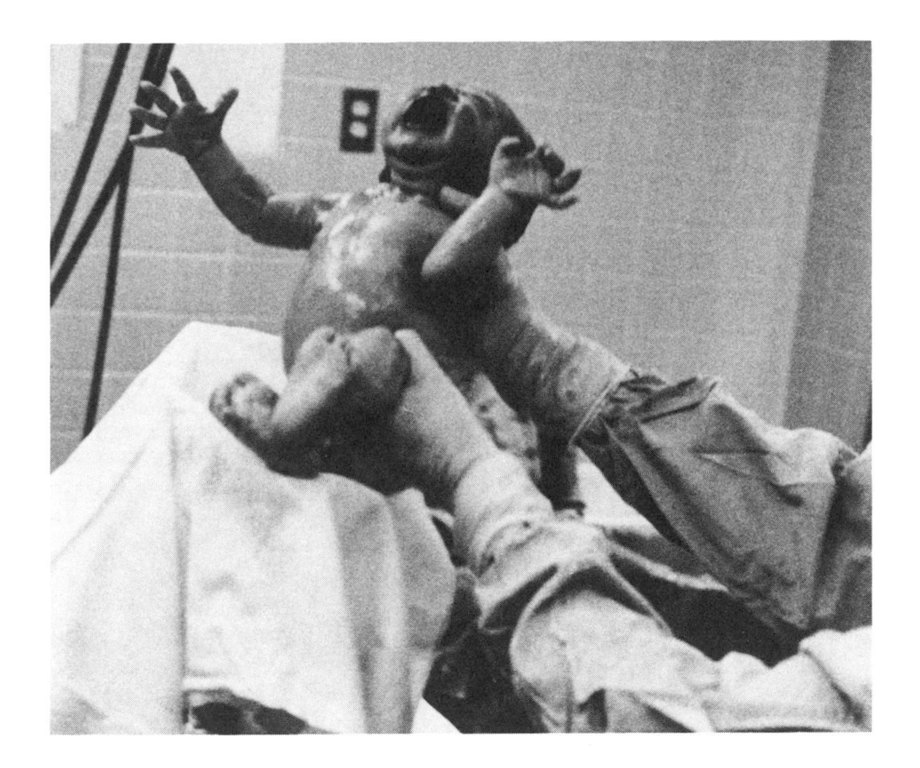

A passage in the Old Testament relates that "God formed man of dust from the ground, and breathed into his nostrils the breath of life, and he became a living being" (Genesis 1:2,9). This biblical verse tells the story of how God breathed life into Adam, known in the Bible as the first human being. It also reflects the fact that even in earliest times, people regarded breathing as the most basic sign of life, looking upon it with awe and a sense of wonder. Throughout history, people have connected breathing with the mysteries of life and death, identifying it with divine powers, magical abilities, and the human spirit.

In an ancient Australian creation myth, for example, a god brought two mud figures to life by breathing into their mouths, noses, and navels. A Middle Eastern myth relates that the first man was created by lesser angels, but that the new being could only creep on the ground until God breathed into it, after which it could walk like a human.

In the ancient South Sea kingdom of Fiji, people with breathing ailments were thought to be losing their souls; magic was used to fasten life into them again. Also in Fiji, people were sacrificed on shore as the new boat of a chief was launched; the dying breaths of the victims were thought to provide "good-luck wind."

Early Romans and Egyptians, too, believed in the mystical powers of human breath and in spirits of the air. The Egyptian vulture-goddess Maut was thought to produce offspring fathered by the wind; in early Rome, a dying person's next of kin had the right to inhale the sufferer's final breath and thus his spirit. This idea is similar to one held by native North Americans; the Algonquians, for example, buried dead children near paths, so that passing young women might breathe in their spirits, which were then thought to be reborn.

Some of these pagan ideas influenced early Christian symbolism. One legend says that the archangel Gabriel's breath caused the Virgin Mary to conceive the child Jesus. Other versions relate that a dove—a being of the air, symbol of the Holy Spirit—announced the birth to Mary.

In the modern world, beliefs about breathing remain the basis for widespread spiritual doctrines and practices. Hinduism, for example, teaches that the mind and breath are identical. Breath control (*pranayama*) is an element of yoga, a form of meditation based on this Hindu belief.

Similarly, in modern medicine, special ways of breathing are used to control some forms of pain. Because anesthetic (pain-killing) drugs may be harmful to unborn babies, for instance, many women in childbirth use breathing techniques to reduce the need for such drugs.

Although magical and religious beliefs about breathing were

common among the earliest peoples, true scientific understanding of the respiratory system has taken many centuries to develop. Even the great Greek doctor Hippocrates (460–359 B.C.E.—*B.C.E.* stands for "before the common era" and is equivalent to B.C.), who was the first to describe a form of disordered breathing known today as Cheyne-Stokes respiration, had no understanding of the reasons behind what he saw, for he knew little of anatomy (body structure) and less of physiology (how the body works).

At the ancient medical school of Alexandria, in Egypt, Eristratus (300–250 B.C.E.) taught that life was caused by a vapor in the breath, which moved to the heart and became a vital spirit, or *pneuma*. His doctrine, called *pneumatism,* was one of the earliest attempts to explain respiration.

Several hundred years later in Rome, Galen of Pergamon (C.E. 129–200—*C.E.* is equivalent to *A.D.* and stands for "common era") devised and recorded a huge medical system, a gathering together of all then current knowledge about the human body. The most respected medical man of his time and for centuries afterward,

The ancient Roman physician Galen, shown here teaching anatomy to medical students, was the first to observe that a spinal-cord injury can destroy a person's ability to breathe.

Galen's extensive studies of anatomy and physiology led him to theorize there were three types of pneuma: one in the breath, one in the blood, and one in the brain. On a more practical level, Galen was the first to observe that a spinal-cord injury can destroy a person's ability to breathe.

With the rise of Christianity, much of the ancient pagan learning was destroyed. In Europe from about C.E. 400 to 1200, few people but Christian monks practiced medicine, and even they did not pursue science. Not until about 1500 did true interest in anatomy and physiology begin reawakening. As the Renaissance progressed, these sciences were revived, and bit by bit facts about human respiration began coming to light.

Leonardo da Vinci (1452–1519) was among the artists of his day who dissected bodies to learn how better to draw and paint the human form. Contrary to widely held beliefs of that time, he discovered that air tubes in the lungs did not make direct contact with blood in the vessels.

Shortly after da Vinci's discoveries, the anatomist Andreas Vesalius (1514–64) performed experiments on the respiratory systems of living animals. During one such experiment he put a tube into the windpipe of an animal, blew into the lungs with a bellows, and proved that an animal can be kept alive with artificial respiration.

More Advanced Theories

Because the blood vessels of the heart and lungs are so intimately connected with one another, the study of the blood's behavior became part of investigations into respiration. By experiment and observation, the English physician William Harvey (1578–1657) found that blood circulated in the body—that instead of blood constantly being created afresh, the same blood went around the body again and again. In 1661, the Italian anatomist Marcello Malpighi described how blood manages to make its circuit, through tiny vessels called *capillaries,* from the smallest arterioles to the smallest venules.

Also during the mid-17th century, investigators in other areas of science, chemistry in particular, began contributing clues to the mysteries of human breathing. In England, Robert Boyle (1627–91) showed that air was not a spirit but a real substance, a material that could be weighed. He demonstrated that when this invisible substance was pumped out of a sealed jar, an animal inside the jar could not breathe. John Mayow (1641–79) showed that one particular substance in air was needed both for a fire to burn and for an animal to breathe.

In 1771 another Englishman, Joseph Priestley, discovered oxygen; soon after, the French chemist Lavoisier (1743–94) found that oxygen was the component of air used by the body. Lavoisier had been studying combustion—the burning of matter—when he learned of the discovery of oxygen. He theorized that in the body, oxygen supported a combustionlike process in the lungs or the blood.

Later, Lavoisier calculated how much oxygen the body used under different conditions and found that the body's oxygen consumption depends upon its temperature, digestion, and the amount of work it is doing. Because of this discovery Lavoisier is known as the pioneer of the study of *metabolism*—the transformation of food into energy that the body's cells can use.

The 18th-century French chemist Lavoisier, shown in this engraving analyzing atmospheric air, discovered that oxygen was the component of air utilized by the body.

By the middle of the 19th century, there was a surge of interest in discovering how oxygen traveled around the body. A German scientist, Eduard Pflueger (1829–1910), showed that metabolism occurs not in the lungs or the blood, but in the body's tissues. The French scientist Claude Bernard (1813–78) found that oxygen is carried to those tissues by red blood cells. Scientists also discovered that oxygen is held in the red blood cell by a substance called *hemoglobin,* and that hemoglobin releases its oxygen and takes up the waste product of metabolism, carbon dioxide, for removal.

One of history's greatest investigators of respiration was England's John Haldane (1860–1936). Haldane developed methods that enabled scientists to learn how much oxygen and carbon dioxide are contained in a person's blood and lungs at any time, and how the body regulates breathing in response to these substances. He also studied the breathing process and the energy the body uses to breathe.

Haldane's work greatly advanced human understanding of respiration, resulting in better methods of oxygen administration and more complete treatment of wounded soldiers during World War I. His work also led to important knowledge about "the bends," an affliction that strikes divers who rise from great ocean depths too quickly, as well as better safety measures for miners.

In the early 1900s, discoveries abounded. One of the most revolutionary of these was the discovery of how oxygen passes from the lungs into the blood. It was known at the time that the wall of the alveolus (the tiny air sac in the lung through which gases pass into and out of the blood) is a very thin membrane; between 1920 and 1923, Sir Joseph Barcroft (1872–1947) conducted a series of experiments to prove that oxygen passed from the lung through the membrane surrounding each alveolus and into the blood by diffusion. That is to say, the oxygen moved from a place where there was more of it (the lung) to a place where there was less (the blood) without having to be "pumped" by any other process.

In his first experiment, Barcroft lived for six days in a glass chamber whose oxygen content was then gradually reduced, periodically having his blood sampled and analyzed for its oxygen content. In the second experiment, Barcroft climbed 14,000 feet to the top of a mountain in Peru and remained there for several months, again allowing his blood to be analyzed. At that time, many people believed that there was an active transport of oxygen from the heart into the blood, but Barcroft proved, by his efforts, that oxygen diffuses from the lung into the blood, rather than being forced into the blood by some unknown process.

While all of these discoveries and experiments were proceeding, the clinical diagnosis (identification in patients) and treatment of disease was also progressing. A Viennese physician named Leopold Auenberger (1722–1809) invented *percussion,* a way of tapping on the chest and using the sound thus produced to diagnose abnormal conditions in the chest and lungs. In 1819, the Breton physician René Laënnec (1781–1826) invented the steth-

An operating room in a German army field hospital during World War I. The wars of the 20th century forced further advances in the area of chest surgery, leading to new and sophisticated surgical techniques.

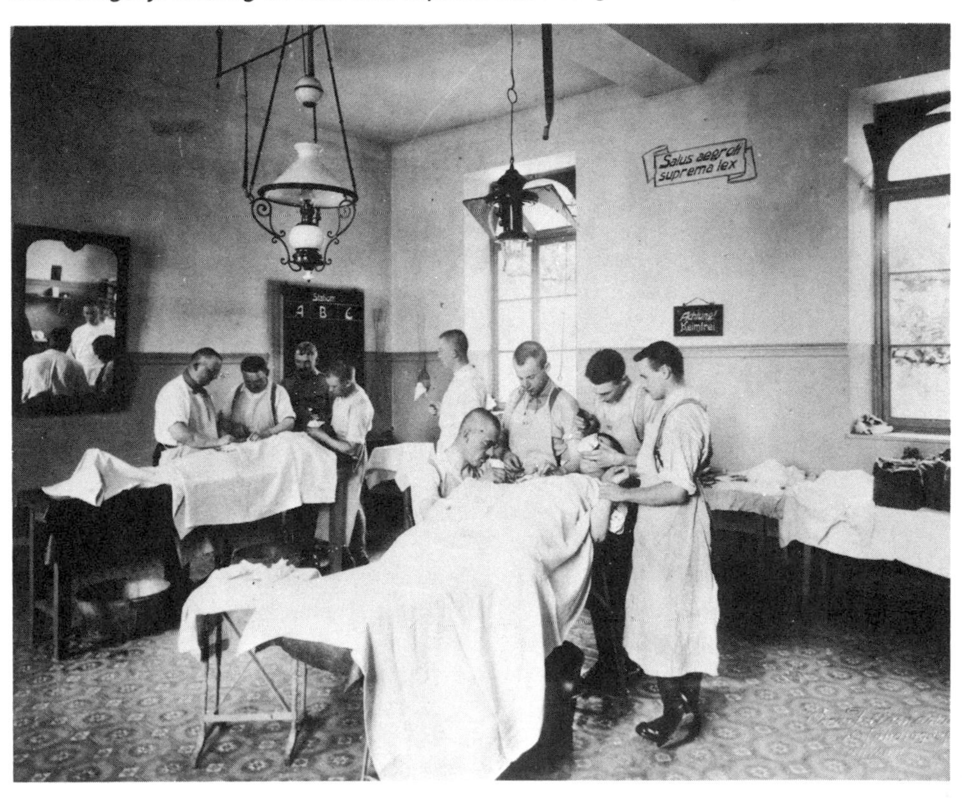

The History of Tuberculosis

During the first half of the 20th century mobile tuberculosis units were sent to schools to test children for the disease.

References to tuberculosis, formerly known as consumption, can be found in both historical accounts and literature throughout the centuries. The disease once afflicted many well-known artists, writers, and musicians. Romantic poet John Keats, for example, died at the age of 25 from tuberculosis. The Brontë sisters, Emily and Charlotte, both wrote their great novels while suffering from the illness. Other well-known tuberculosis patients included poet Percy Bysshe Shelley; composer Frédéric Chopin; painter Paul Gauguin; authors Robert Louis Stevenson, Washington Irving, and Anton Chekhov; and First Lady Eleanor Roosevelt.

Tuberculosis is actually caused by a germ that can be carried through dust and air. Although it can attack other areas of the body (the brain and bones, for example), the disease usually settles in the lungs, where its rod-shaped bacteria (microorganisms) destroy and eat holes through the soft tissue. Pulmonary tuberculosis (or tuberculosis that has settled in a person's lungs) is contagious and can be passed on through a cough or a sneeze.

Some 19th-century treatments for the disease included drinking elephant's blood, spending time by the sea, and touching the hand of a reigning monarch. During the late 1880s the medical community came to believe that fresh air and relaxation were beneficial to the TB patient; consequently, the use of sanitoriums, where patients were assured of fresh air, rest, and care, became the preferred method of treatment.

At that same time, city councils in the eastern part of the United States began to approve funds to send tuberculosis patients to recover in the West. Soon, there were colonies of tuberculosis patients living in tent or wagon communities outside of Denver, Los Angeles, and other southwestern cities. Although many councils claimed that they were sending the TB patients out to the West simply to restore their health, it was obvious that by ridding themselves of those afflicted with the disease they were lessening the risk of contagion within their own cities.

The early 1900s witnessed the creation of open-air schools for children who had or were suspected of having the disease. Classrooms in these schools were equipped with large, open windows, or were outside all together. During the mid-20th century, mobile tuberculosis units were dispatched throughout the United States, taking chest X rays and informing employees and schoolchildren about the dangers of the disease. But by 1944 nearly 126,000 new cases of tuberculosis were being reported each year.

In 1944, the drug streptomycin, discovered by Dr. Selman Waksman, began to control the tuberculosis problem. Combined with the early detection of the disease made possible by routine skin tests, the use of streptomycin led to a dramatic decline in the number of cases of tuberculosis. As a result the disease ceased to be the number-one killer in the United States.

In the late 1980s, however, the number of tuberculosis patients began to increase once again. The disease reappeared in large cities, among the poor and homeless living in unsanitary conditions. It also found easy prey among people with AIDS, a fatal breakdown of the immune system caused by a virus that leaves the victim open to a variety of other diseases and infections.

As of July 1988, according to the Centers for Disease Control in Atlanta, nearly 22,000 people contracted tuberculosis every year, and about 1,800 died from it. Sadly, this latest epidemic indicates that even in an era of sophisticated medical technology and miraculous cures, inadequate living conditions and poor health care can lead to a resurgence of a disease once considered obsolete.

oscope, a device for hearing air movements in the lungs (as well as sounds made by other organs in the chest).

Also during the early 19th century, physicians were just beginning to use surgery to treat tuberculosis in the lungs. This surgical procedure, called artificial pneumothorax, was a simple puncture into the chest and was used to collapse the lung on the punctured side in the hope of stopping the disease. Further prog-

In 1946, a 12-year-old polio patient confined to an iron lung reads a greeting card from his scout troop. The polio epidemic of the 1940s and 1950s impelled the invention of the mechanical respirator, or iron lung.

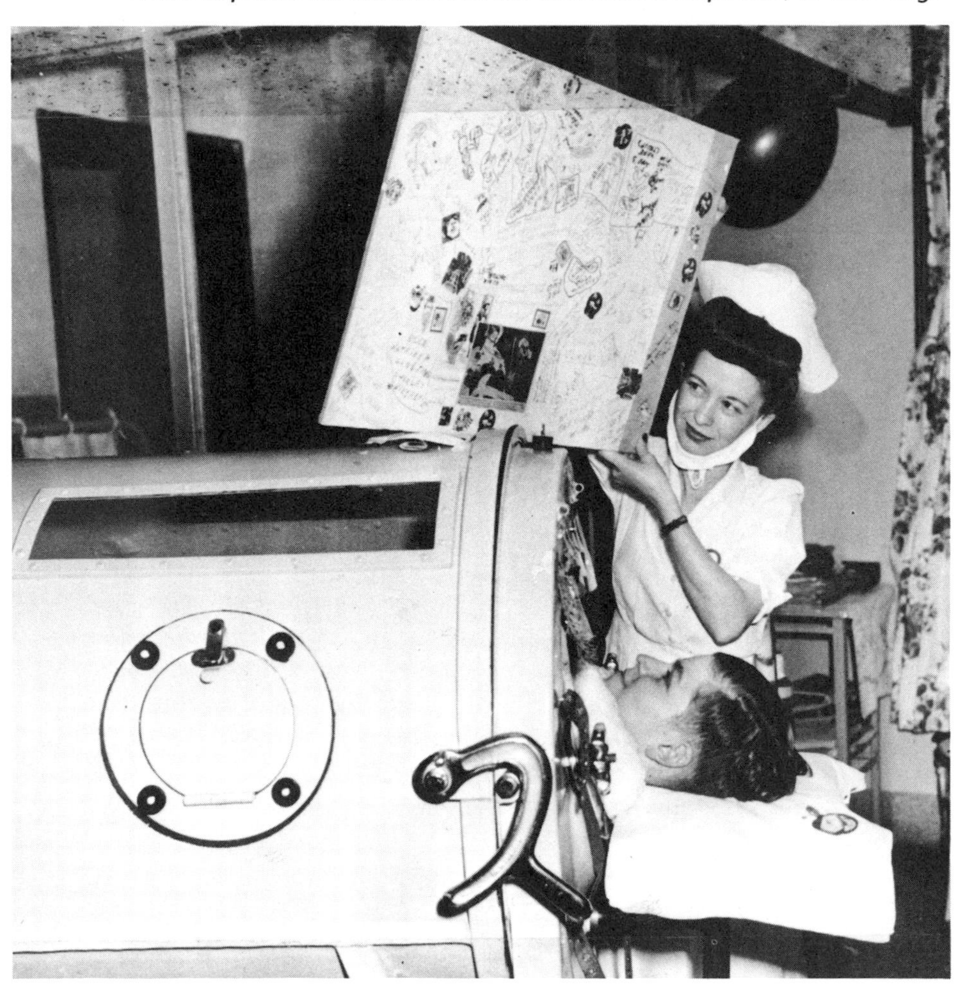

ress in chest surgery did not occur until World War I, when the chest wounds of soldiers made surgeons willing to try desperate measures to save lives and often led to surprising new surgical successes.

Even earlier, however, one man had made a mark in the annals of successful chest surgery. The Scotsman Sir William Macewen (1848–1924) was a gifted surgeon, best known for the surgical operations he performed on the brain, and one of the first surgeons to use steam and boiling to cleanse instruments and bandages. In 1895 Macewen was asked to perform chest surgery to ease the pain of a patient's lung abscess; in an unprecedented operation, Macewen removed one entire lung from the man—who lived in good health for 45 years afterward.

By the turn of the century, medical science had progressed still further. The germs causing tuberculosis and some pneumonias had been found and identified. In 1895, the German scientist Wilhelm Roentgen (1845–1923) discovered X rays, which by 1922 were being used to find and diagnose diseases of the lungs. The wars of the early 20th century forced further advances in chest surgery, while the poliomyelitis (infantile paralysis) epidemic of the 1940s and early 1950s impelled the invention of the mechanical respirator to support breathing in paralyzed patients. High-altitude flying during World War II spurred the development of the Bird respirator, which let pilots breathe pressurized oxygen and thus fly higher than humans had ever flown before.

Between the 1950s and the 1980s, knowledge about the respiratory system reached a "critical mass," exploding into a new era of modern research and disease treatment. New antibiotic drugs were developed and refined for treating germ-caused lung diseases such as tuberculosis and pneumonia. Air pollution was recognized as a threat to health, and laws combating it were passed. Smoking was found to cause lung disease, and the prevention and cure of cigarette-related ailments began. And in a stunning display of medical and surgical expertise, the first heart/lung organ transplant surgery was performed in the early 1980s.

Much remains to be learned about the human respiratory system. Breathing is one of the most essential functions of the human body, and physicians and scientists continue to seek more knowledge about it. As a result, young people living today have a better chance than at any other time in history of enjoying a long life and better health, benefits partly made possible by modern medical and scientific knowledge of breathing and the human respiratory system.

• • • •

CHAPTER 2

HOW LIVING THINGS BREATHE

As we already know, the human body can only survive for about three minutes without air. This is because the body's cells use up oxygen and give off carbon dioxide during *metabolism.*

Metabolism is the process of chemical change that living cells must constantly engage in for the purpose of supplying energy to themselves. Metabolism may be imagined as a tiny fire, constantly burning fuel (food), giving off heat (energy), and creating ashes (waste). Like a fire, the metabolism of a living cell consumes oxygen as it turns fuel to energy; without oxygen the fires of metabolism—and the cell itself—would die. Similarly, cells die if the waste products of metabolism are not removed, much as a fire can be smothered by its own ashes.

Thus oxygen must constantly be supplied to living cells, and carbon dioxide must constantly be removed from them. The process of doing so is called *respiration*. Depending on their special needs and environments, different kinds of living creatures have different methods of respiration.

The one-celled water organisms called protozoans, for example, have no special organs for breathing; instead, they breathe passively (without taking any deliberate action) by *osmosis*. In osmosis, oxygen moves from an area where it is plentiful—outside of the protozoan—to the inside of the protozoan by passing through the protozoan's *cell wall* (the outer membrane that surrounds the organism). Carbon dioxide moves out of the protozoan and back into the surroundings by the same simple process. No matter what gas or membrane is involved, osmosis always works in this same way: A substance moves across a membrane from a place where it is more abundant to a place where it is less abundant.

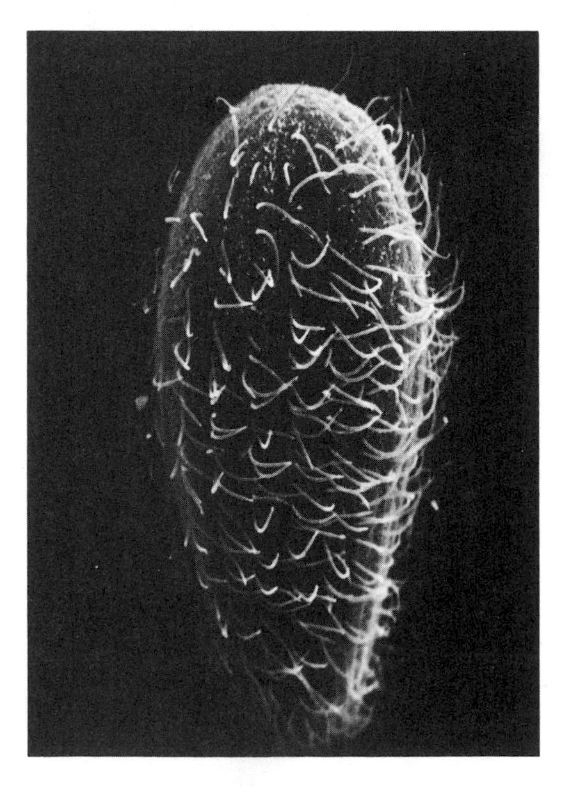

A magnification of a protozoan, a one-celled water organism that breathes passively, or by osmosis.

Fish breathe through gills, or tissuelike membranes, that take in oxygen from the water that flows over them.

Larger, more complex creatures require more sophisticated respiratory systems, tailored to their environments and activities. Insects that live on land, for example, breathe through holes called *spiracles* in their chests and abdomens. The holes lead to tubes called *tracheae,* which carry air deep inside the insects' bodies. Spiders, which are arachnids, have "book lungs," leaflets like the pages of a book, in slits in their abdomens. The book lungs allow air to flow into the spiders' bodies, where the oxygen passes into the blood by osmosis, and the carbon dioxide passes out.

Insects that spend part of their lives underwater may have *gills,* membranes through which oxygen passes by osmosis from the surrounding water (in which the oxygen is dissolved) into the insect's blood. Or they may depend on "bubble diving": trapping an air bubble under a wing, then breathing from the bubble while completing underwater activities.

A beetle called the water boatman is expert in the bubble diving technique, while one species of spider, *Argyroneta aquatica,* takes bubble diving a step further: It lives its life underwater by build-

Spiders have "book lungs," or leaflets like the pages of a book, which allow air to flow into the spider's body. Once in the body, the oxygen enters the spider's blood through osmosis.

ing a sort of "diving-bell" spiderweb, then filling this aquatic home with air bubbles that it captures at the water's surface.

Insects such as mayflies and dragonflies spend their early lives as water-dwelling *nymphs* that breathe through gills; when these insects mature, they develop spiracles and tracheae to adapt to air breathing. But many invertebrates (organisms without backbones) spend their whole lives in the water and depend entirely on gills for obtaining oxygen and disposing of carbon dioxide.

Starfish and sea urchins breathe through their feet, for that is where their gills are located. Clams and other mollusks use millions of tiny *cilia* (hairlike structures) that whip about constantly to bring in water that carries oxygen to their gills and at the same time carries food to their mouths. Crustaceans such as shrimp and crabs have special legs that move oxygen-rich water over their gills.

A fish is a gilled vertebrate (an animal with a backbone). Fish can open and close their gills by raising and lowering the gills' bony covering, the *operculum*. Inside the gill chamber, fish gills are thin, tissuelike membranes folded many times over. The folds, called *lamellae,* allow a large amount of gill surface area to fit into the small space of the gill chamber (you can test this by trying to fit a piece of unfolded notebook paper into your pocket; it will not fit until you fold it). The extent of the surface area is important, because the more surface area a gill has, the more oxygen-rich water can flow over it at one time. The crayfish, for example, has gills which, through osmosis, take in oxygen and expel carbon dioxide.

Amphibians such as frogs use both gills and air-breathing lungs at different times in their lives. Immature frogs (tadpoles) breathe with gills but also through their skin, especially the skin of their large tails. As they change into mature frogs (through the shape-changing process called *metamorphosis*), they lose their gills and tails and develop air-breathing lungs. Most frogs, however, retain some ability to breathe through skin that is exposed to water. Some frogs even divide the work of respiration, taking up oxygen mainly through their lungs and excreting carbon dioxide primarily through their skin.

Unlike amphibians, reptiles such as lizards and snakes breathe entirely with their lungs. Turtles, encased in rigid shells, face a special breathing challenge: While most air-breathing creatures use energy only to inhale and simply relax to exhale, the shell-bound turtle must use energy both to inhale and exhale.

Because turtles are encased in a rigid shell, they face special breathing problems. In order to overcome these problems, they must expend energy to both inhale and exhale.

Birds, too, face special challenges in the task of respiration, because they need a great deal of energy to fly and to maintain their bodies' heat. This means they must eat a lot of food and use a great deal of oxygen to turn this large volume of food into needed energy.

To meet this challenge, the respiratory system of a bird is about twice the size of that of a similar-sized mammal. Also, birds' lungs inflate more completely than do those of mammals, and birds' rate of breathing increases enormously during flight. Pigeons, for instance, breathe 20 times faster during flight than they do at rest. Birds also use their respiratory systems for communication, controlling both the rate and size of breaths to produce their characteristic songs.

Humans and Other Mammals

Mammals (warm-blooded animals that nourish their young with milk—such as chipmunks, elephants, and humans) breathe air through lungs by a process called *negative-pressure inspiration.* This process will be explained more fully later, but briefly and simply it works like this: (1) Muscles in the chest and abdomen contract; (2) The chest cavity enlarges; (3) The lungs expand and air flows into them (inhalation); (4) The chest and abdominal muscles relax and the chest cavity shrinks; and (5) As the chest cavity shrinks, air is pushed out of the lungs (exhalation).

Before birth, mammals do not breathe at all. Instead, the unborn mammal's need for oxygen, nourishment, and waste removal is met by its mother, through the umbilical cord that connects the mother and her offspring. Meanwhile, the unborn mammal's respiratory system grows and develops, readying itself for the moment when the newborn creature will take its first breath of air.

In human beings, the respiratory system begins to form just a few weeks after the infant is conceived, as an outpouching of the digestive tract. By the time the fetus has developed for 16 weeks, its lungs have grown so that almost all of the air tubes (bronchi) of the lung are in place. One month later, the lungs' blood vessels have begun to develop, and 2 months after that—when the fetus is 28 weeks old—the lungs and vessels are mature enough to support life outside the mother's womb (the organ that carries and nourishes the unborn infant).

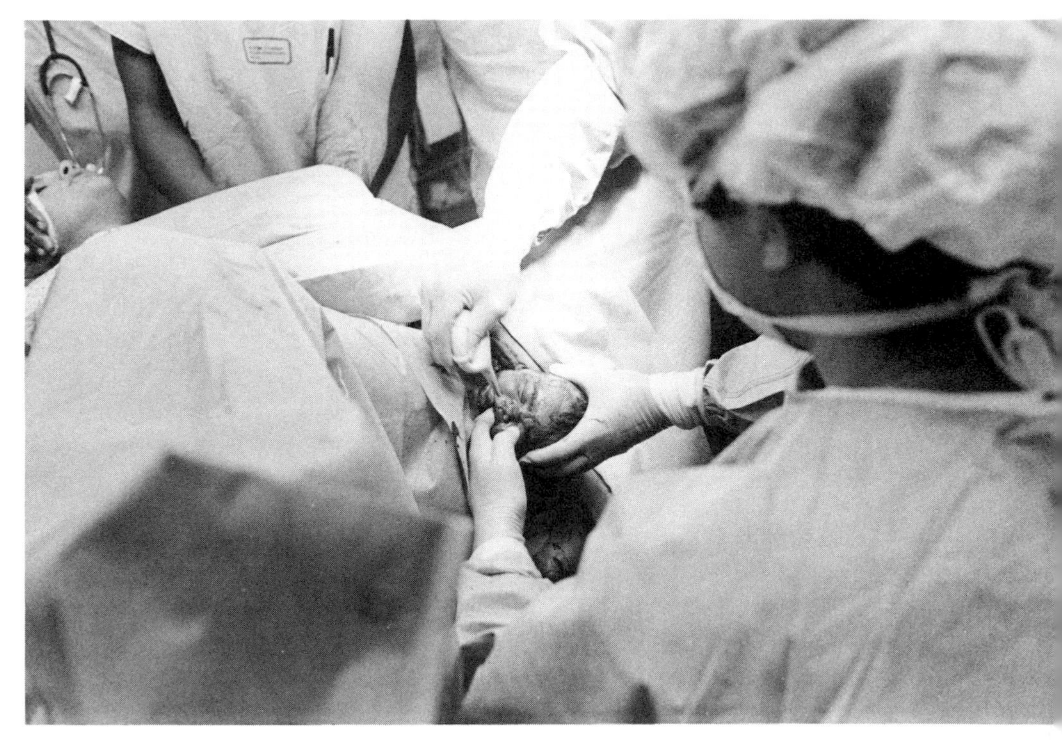

A baby emerges from the womb as a physician suctions the mucus from his nose and mouth. The first breath a baby must take is the hardest, because at birth his lungs are filled with fluid.

In the moments following a human infant's birth, the infant must learn to adapt to its new, independent existence. No longer does the umbilical cord supply it with oxygen and nutrients from the mother and carry off waste products such as carbon dioxide for the mother's body to remove. Now the newborn must perform these functions for itself—and it must do so effectively within moments of birth, or it will not survive.

The newborn's nervous system quickly triggers its first breath—a breath that may be the most difficult of its whole life, because at birth its lungs are nearly filled with fluid. With its first exhalation the infant expels a large amount of this fluid; its next few breaths gradually become easier.

One substance that helps the newborn adapt to its new, air-breathing life is called *pulmonary surfactant.* Produced by the infant's lungs before birth, this surfactant is contained in the fluid that coats the *alveoli,* the tiny air sacs in the lung. Once an air sac is opened by an infant's first breath, the surfactant, by reducing the surface tension of the fluid lining the air sac, helps the air sac to hold its open shape, so that it does not collapse when the infant exhales. The surfactant holds the air sac open by creating, in each sac, a bubble that can be likened to a soap bubble.

Surface tension is the force that holds the surface shape of a fluid. For example, most people have seen water bugs walk across the surface of a pond or lake. This is possible because the weight of a water bug is not enough to break the surface tension of the water.

While the new infant's lungs are opening, its heart must also adapt to the new situation of air breathing. Before birth, its heart pumped blood, but the oxygen that entered this blood came from the mother's lungs, which also removed carbon dioxide from the blood. But after birth, the infant's own heart and lungs must work together: to obtain oxygen from air, to transfer it from the lungs to the blood, and to pump it out to the body's cells where it is needed. Meanwhile, carbon dioxide must be removed from the infant's body cells, moved via the blood to the lungs, and exhaled from the body.

In practice, this means that the heart must function as two systems. From the moment of birth onward, the pumping of the heart's right side will power the *pulmonary circulation,* sending blood that comes into the heart from the rest of the body to the lungs where it can take up oxygen and discharge carbon dioxide. At the same time, the heart's left side will power the *systemic circulation,* sending the oxygen-rich, carbon dioxide-cleansed blood that comes back to the heart from the lungs out to the body's cells, where oxygen is delivered and carbon dioxide removed.

We will look more closely at the intricate parts of the respiratory system. What are the basic parts? How do they work? How do they perform two of life's basic chores: oxygen uptake and carbon dioxide disposal? In Chapter 3 we will find the answers to these questions, as well as a better understanding of the vital function of the human respiratory system.

• • • •

CHAPTER 3

THE HUMAN RESPIRATORY SYSTEM

To carry oxygen and carbon dioxide on their vital journeys to and from the lungs and cells, the mammalian body has developed specialized structures: the various parts of the respiratory system. The human respiratory system consists of the nose, the *pharynx* (throat), the *larynx* (voice box), the *trachea* (windpipe), the *bronchi* (air tubes), and the *lungs*.

The outermost part of the system is the *nose*. It warms, cleanses, and humidifies the air that the lungs breathe in. The entrance to the nose is the *vestibule;* inside, the right and left *nasal cavities* are divided by a thin membrane, the nasal *septum*. The tissue inside the nose, like the tissue that lines most of the respiratory system, is of a special type called *ciliated columnar epithelium*.

Contained within this tissue are cells called *goblet cells* that produce *mucus,* a sticky fluid that catches dust and bacteria and prevents them from reaching the lungs. Tiny hairlike projections on the surface of the columnar epithelium, the *cilia,* move the mucus and any impurities it has captured toward the throat, where it is expelled or swallowed.

The upper part of the two nasal cavities contains the endings of the *olfactory nerves,* which are responsible for our sense of smell. The act of sniffing moves air up to these nerve endings; the olfactory nerves carry impulses from the nerve endings to the brain, which tells us whether we are smelling roses or rotten eggs.

The *pharynx* is the chamber behind and below the nasal cavity. The lower, frontal part of the pharynx, the *oropharynx,* contains the tongue and teeth and is part of the digestive system. The upper part, through which air passes from the nose on its way to the lungs, is the *nasopharynx.* The *soft palate* (the roof of the back of the mouth) separates the oropharynx from the nasopharynx. Hanging down from the back of the soft palate is a small, soft tag of flesh that is called the *uvula.*

From the sides of the nasopharynx, the *eustachian tubes* lead to the inner ears; by allowing air to pass back and forth from the nasopharynx, these tubes stabilize the air pressure on the eardrums, but they may also allow respiratory infection to spread to the ears. This is why a cold sometimes develops into an ear infection. The *tonsils* and *adenoids* lie at the back of the nasopharynx; these glands, made up of *lymph tissue,* are part of the immune system, which defends the body against infection.

Below the pharynx lies the *larynx,* or voice box. It has a "lid," a flap of tissue called the *epiglottis* that covers the larynx when swallowing occurs, so that no food or drink enters the airway. Inside the larynx are the wide membranes of the *vocal cords*; the area in which the vocal cords are found is the *glottis.* Some muscles of the larynx can be controlled voluntarily to lengthen or shorten the cords and alter the diameter of the larynx, thereby permitting speaking and singing. But inhaling automatically widens the opening (known as the *rima glottidis*) between the vocal cords so that air may pass between them easily.

The outer structure of the larynx is made up of *cartilage rings.* (Cartilage is a flexible, bonelike tissue, but not as stiff as bone. The tip of the nose is made of cartilage.) The largest cartilage of

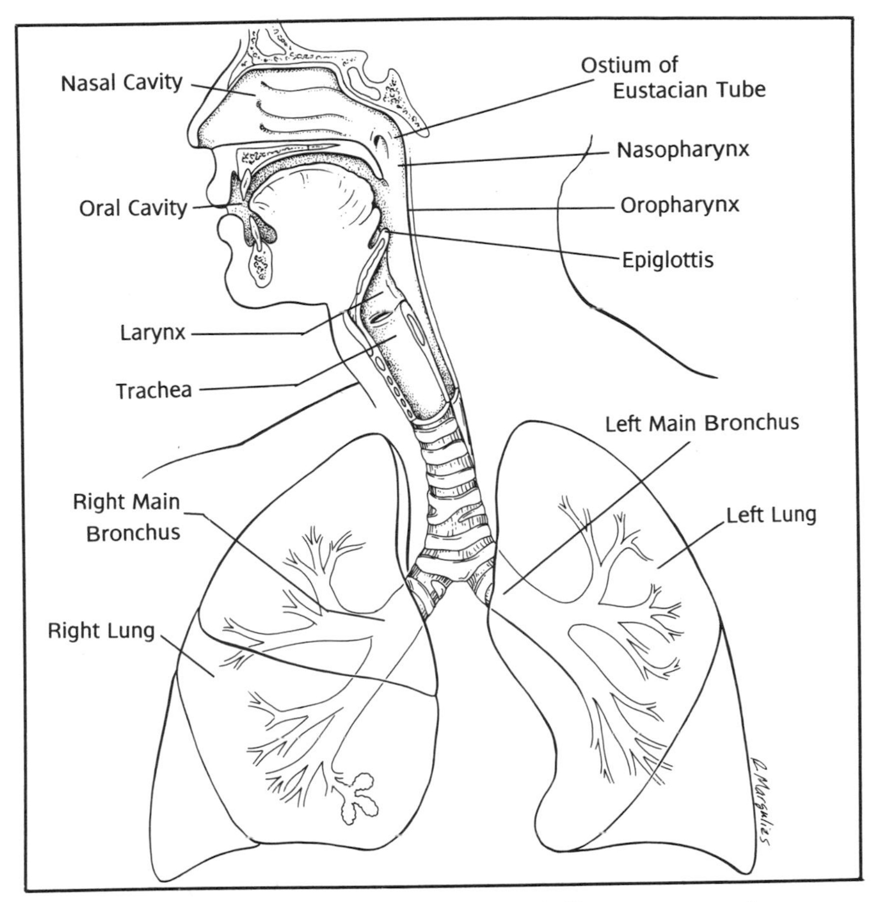

Figure 1: The Human Respiratory System. *Unlike many organisms, mammals, including humans, have an extremely complex system for taking in oxygen and distributing it throughout the body.*

the larynx is the *thyroid cartilage,* visible on the front of the neck as the Adam's apple in men. At the bottom of the larynx, the *cricoid cartilage* lies just above the *trachea,* or windpipe.

The trachea is a tube lined with *mucous membrane* (a tissue somewhat like that in the nose, which can produce mucus) and is held in shape by about 20 horseshoe-shaped cartilage rings covered by a tough, elastic membrane. At the back of the trachea is a layer of *smooth muscle* that can pull the open ends of the cartilage rings together to decrease the diameter of the trachea. If foreign matter enters the trachea, these muscles constrict to prevent the offending material from slipping deeper into the airway.

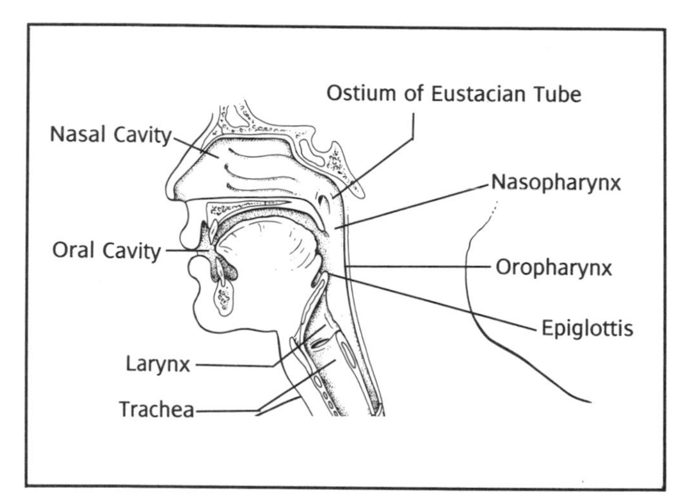

Figure 2: The Upper Respiratory System. *Air enters the body through either the nasal or oral cavity, where it is cleansed, warmed, and humidified. It then passes through either the nasopharynx or oropharynx before moving through the epiglottis into the larynx, and finally into the trachea, or windpipe. From the trachea, the air moves into the lungs.*

In an adult, the trachea is about five inches long. The upper half of the its length is in the throat; the rest extends down into the thorax (chest). About two inches below the *suprasternal notch* (the bony notch at the top center of the chest) the trachea divides into two branches: the *mainstem bronchi.*

The mainstem bronchi are each about two inches long and, like the trachea, are held open by cartilage rings. Each mainstem bronchus enters a lung at the lung's *hilus* (entry point). The blood vessels and nerves also enter the lung at the hilus.

In the chest cavity, the lungs are divided by the *mediastinum* (the middle area inside the chest). The mediastinum contains the heart, esophagus (food tube), trachea, and the body's main blood vessels under the long, flat middle bone of the chest called the *sternum.*

The lungs themselves, lying on either side of the mediastinum, are covered by a tough, slippery membrane called the *pulmonary pleura.* A portion of this membrane also lines the chest cavity, where it is called the *parietal pleura.*

Deep grooves or furrows in the lungs mark their division into *lobes,* or parts. The left lung comprises two lobes; the right lung has three. This is because the left lung must share its half of the chest cavity with the heart. In the lungs, the mainstem bronchi branch again to form *lobar bronchi,* one leading to each lobe.

In the lungs, the bronchi are completely encircled by smooth muscle instead of having it only in their rear walls, like the mainstem bronchi and the trachea. Large bronchi in the lungs also have plates of cartilage embedded in their walls, instead of cartilage rings running around them.

In the lobes of the lungs, the bronchi divide once again, into *segmental bronchi,* of which there are 10 in the right lung and 9 in the left lung. A segmental bronchus carries air to a section of the lung called a segment. The segments are important because the thin membranes between them can help keep infections and other diseases from spreading within the lung.

After the bronchi have divided into segmental bronchi, they divide as many as 20 more times, eventually forming tiny tubes only four-hundredths of an inch in diameter. These very small tubes, which like the rest of the bronchi are encircled by smooth muscle and lined with mucous membrane, are the *terminal bronchioles*. The shape of the entire bronchial system is like the shape of a tree, with the trunk being like the trachea and the tiniest branches like the terminal bronchioles. In fact, the bronchial system as a whole is often called the *pulmonary tree.*

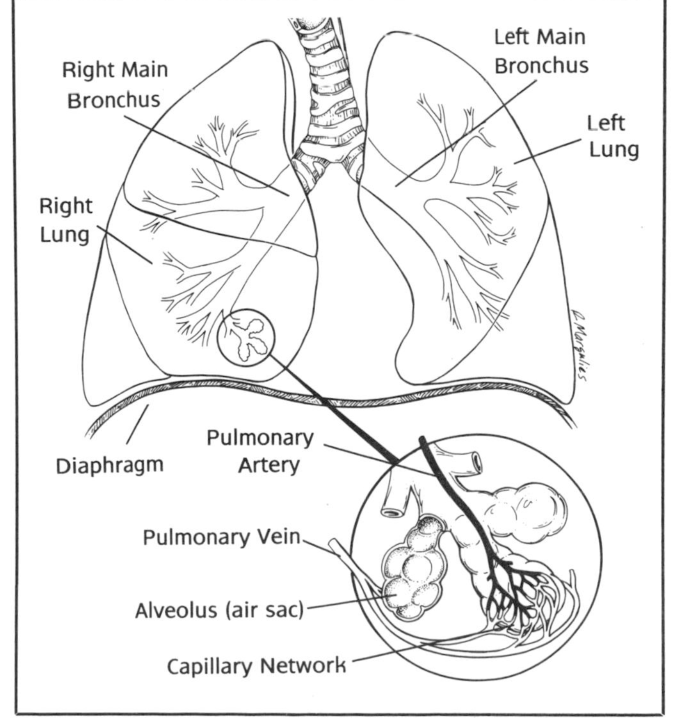

Figure 3: The Lungs. *The smallest part of each lung is the alveolus (enlarged here to show details). Each lung contains between 300- to 400-million alveoli. It is through the alveolar membrane that oxygen diffuses into the blood, to be carried to the cells.*

Each of the terminal bronchioles—there are from 20 to 80 thousand of them in the lung—ends in a berry-shaped structure called an *acinus*. In the acinus lie the *respiratory bronchioles*. These smallest of all bronchioles lead to the *alveolar ducts* and thence to the very ends of the bronchi, where the *alveoli* are located.

The alveoli are the tiny, thin-walled air sacs of the lung. Each lung contains from 300- to 400-million alveoli. It is through the *alveolar membrane* that oxygen diffuses by osmosis out of the lung and into the blood, to be carried to the cells. It is also through this membrane that carbon dioxide diffuses in the opposite direction, from the blood to the lungs, from which it is exhaled. Later we will look more closely at the way in which oxygen and carbon dioxide get in and out of the alveoli, how they are carried in the blood, and their roles in cell metabolism.

Other Body Systems Aid Respiration

The respiratory system does not do all the work of respiration alone. Other systems of the body also contribute to the task of breathing. The *diaphragm*, for instance, is a sheetlike muscle that separates the chest from the abdomen. When the diaphragm contracts, it moves downward into the abdomen. This enlarges the chest cavity, causing air to rush into the newly enlarged space and fill the lungs.

The ribs and muscles in the chest walls also contract to help enlarge the chest cavity; when they relax, the cavity shrinks to cause exhalation. When breathing is labored, muscles in the shoulders and neck may join in the work of respiration; these muscles are called the *accessory* muscles of breathing.

The nervous system helps provide the stimulus to breathe, as do carotid and aortic bodies, special organs in the blood vessels that sense when the blood needs more oxygen or is carrying too much carbon dioxide.

For proper respiration, the parts of the respiratory system must work well individually and together. Furthermore, their actions must be coordinated with the rest of the body. In the next chapter we will trace the ways in which the parts of the respiratory system and the other parts of the body cooperate to produce a single breath.

• • • •

CHAPTER 4

HOW BREATHING HAPPENS

Breathing is one of the body's automatic functions—it happens without our having to think about it. At first glance, the process seems fairly simple: Air goes into our lungs and then comes out again.

In fact, however, the real purpose of breathing is a bit more complicated than simply to move air in and out of our lungs. The way in which breathing happens is also more complex than it may seem to us while we are doing it.

The breathing process can be understood more easily when we understand its deeper purpose: We breathe to get oxygen into our blood and to get carbon dioxide out. As we have already seen, our cells take up oxygen from the blood and dump waste carbon dioxide into it.

It makes sense, then, that our blood should carry a great deal of oxygen, so that the cells can pick it up easily. It should not, however, carry a great deal of carbon dioxide, so that the cells will have a place to dump their waste.

This is, in fact, the way in which the body works: It senses how much oxygen and carbon dioxide the blood is carrying. If the blood contains too much carbon dioxide, or too little oxygen, the body automatically breathes more rapidly or deeply to supply it with more oxygen and carry off more waste carbon dioxide.

Oxygen and Carbon Dioxide in the Blood

The oxygen content of the blood is sensed by groups of special cells called the *carotid body* and the *aortic body*. The carotid body is located in a large blood vessel called the *carotid artery,* in the neck. The aortic body is inside another blood vessel, the *aorta,* which is the main vessel leading from the heart to the body. When the blood flowing past these groups of special cells contains too little oxygen, the aortic and carotid bodies send messages to the brain, triggering it to increase the breathing rate.

The carbon dioxide content of the blood is sensed in areas of the brain called the *respiratory centers.* It is believed that there are at least four such centers in the brain: the inspiratory center, the expiratory center, the apneustic center, and the pneumotaxic center.

How these respiratory centers work is not precisely understood. We do, however, know that when the carbon dioxide content of the blood is raised or lowered, chemical changes occur inside the cells of the respiratory centers. These changes then result in faster or slower breathing.

Inhalation and Exhalation

To begin a breath, the brain sends a message down the spinal cord to the *phrenic nerve,* which is connected to the diaphragm. At the same time, the muscles between the ribs contract, moving them outward. The upper ribs are moved by the *intercostal muscles,* and the sternum, the bone at the front of the chest to which the ribs are attached, moves outward as well.

If we think of the diaphragm as the bottom wall of the chest cavity, and of the ribs as its side walls, we can see that, at the beginning of a breath, the bottom wall of the chest cavity moves downward and the side walls move outward, away from the lungs inside the cavity. The chest cavity is enlarging.

Before this breath began, the chest wall was pressing on the lungs. That is, it was exerting *positive pressure* on them. But now the chest wall, moving away from the lungs, exerts the opposite kind of pressure: *negative pressure.* You can see negative pressure in action if you put a straw in a glass of water and suck on it. Water flows upward into the straw, which has been suddenly emptied of air by your sucking. You are exerting negative pressure on the water.

The outward motion of the chest wall exerts this same kind of negative pressure on the lung—that is, it "sucks" the sides of the lung outward. When this happens it creates more room inside the lungs. The result is that air begins flowing into the newly enlarged space—in through the nose, down the windpipe, and

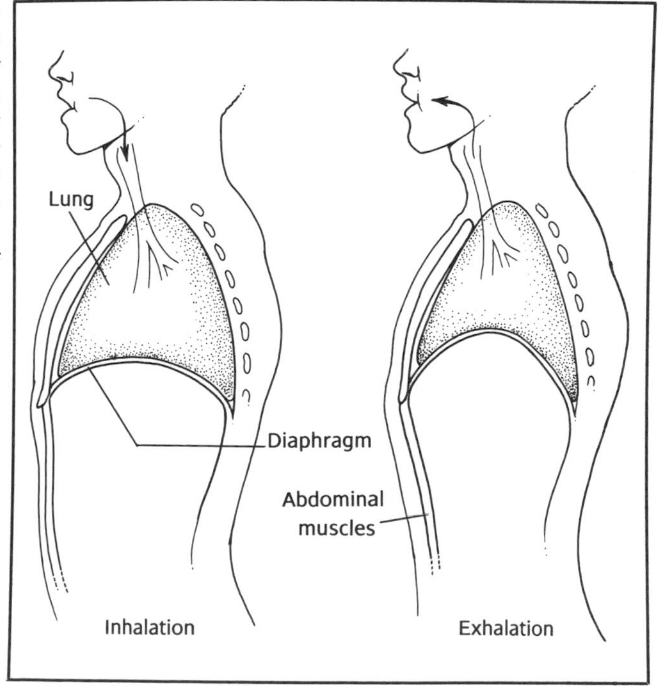

Figure 4: Inhalation/ Exhalation. *When a person inhales, his chest cavity expands to allow his lungs to fill completely with air. The flow of air into the lungs stops when the pressure of the air inside the lungs equals the pressure of the air outside the body.*

into the lungs. As air continues flowing into the lungs, it inflates them, filling the tiny alveoli at the ends of the bronchioles.

Air will keep flowing into the lungs until the air pressure inside them equals the pressure of the atmosphere outside the body—that is, when the newly enlarged space inside the chest cavity (and inside the lungs) is completely filled with air. At this point, the air flow into the lungs stops. The lungs have been inflated, and the first part of a breath, the inhalation phase, is completed.

Most of the events of inhalation are active; the body must use energy in order to breathe in. Transmitting the nervous impulses that stimulate a breath, for example, and contracting the muscles of respiration are both activities that use energy.

Lifting the weight of the chest to expand it takes energy, too; the chest's weight is a *resistance*. Also, in order for the lungs to inflate, they must stretch. Stretching them—overcoming their resistance—is another part of the work of breathing. In addition, as the lungs inflate, their outer surfaces move against the inner surfaces of the chest wall. If it were not for the moist, slippery pulmonary and parietal pleura, moving the lungs against the wall of the chest might take a lot of work, because a great deal of resistance to the movement could occur in the form of friction between the lungs and the chest wall.

To imagine this kind of resistance, think of ice-skating. The skate slides easily on the ice; there is little resistance. Now imagine the skate hitting a patch of sand: The sudden stop is caused by increased resistance.

Finally, air flow itself does not occur effortlessly. Anything that flows through a tube meets a certain amount of resistance because its molecules "bump" against each other and the sides of the tube.

The work the body does to overcome all these resistances is called the work of breathing. By contrast, exhalation is a passive process; to exhale, all the body must do is relax. To understand why exhaling can be a passive event, imagine a spring. Stretching the spring is like inhaling, because to do so you must exert force on the spring (as in the contraction of the respiratory muscles that permits breathing), and because when the spring is stretched, it is bigger (as is the chest cavity following contraction of the respiratory muscles). But when you let go of the spring, it snaps back to its original, contracted shape, and the lungs and chest wall behave in the same way at the end of inhalation. They are elastic, and once the respiratory muscles relax, the chest wall contracts back into its original, smaller shape, just as a spring returns to its unstretched shape.

Exhalation occurs when the respiratory muscles relax and the chest "springs back" to its unexpanded, unstretched shape. The diaphragm rises upward into its uncontracted position, the ribs move inward, and the sternum moves to a lower position. The chest cavity, enlarged a few moments earlier, returns to its smaller size.

As the chest cavity becomes smaller, its walls exert pressure on the lungs, forcing them to occupy a smaller space. As the lungs are pressed inward, and as their own stretchiness, or elasticity, causes them to "snap back" to their unexpanded shape, air is forced out from the alveoli through the bronchi and trachea, past the larynx, into the nasopharynx, and out the nose or mouth.

When exhalation has ended, the respiratory system is ready to start the whole cycle again. But exhalation does not empty the lungs entirely. If it did, the alveoli would collapse, greatly increasing the work required for the body to inhale for the next breath. To understand this, imagine blowing up a balloon. You need to blow very hard into the balloon at first, to get it to expand that first little bit. But after the balloon is slightly expanded, inflating it is easier, and you no longer need to blow as hard.

Another reason why the lungs do not completely deflate is that blood is always circulating through them, picking up oxygen and dropping off carbon dioxide. If the lungs were empty part of the time, they would contain no oxygen for the blood to pick up, and the journey of the blood would be wasted during that "empty time."

In fact, even if a person breathes out as much air as possible, about one-fifth of the lung's air capacity still remains filled. This volume, called the *residual volume,* cannot be exhaled no matter how hard a person tries. Therefore, the blood's journey through the lungs is always a fully useful one: It can pick up oxygen and get rid of carbon dioxide at all times, not only during inhalation.

Although we have now seen how air gets into and out of the lungs, that is really only half the journey. Somehow, oxygen must get from the lungs to the blood, and from blood into the cells where it is used. At the same time, carbon dioxide must travel in the other direction: from the cells to the blood, and from the blood into the lungs and out of the body.

In the next chapter we will examine this "invisible" part of respiration by traveling with a molecule of oxygen as it moves from the lung into the blood, and from the bloodstream into a cell. Once we have seen how the cell uses oxygen in its metabolism, we will take the reverse trip with a carbon dioxide molecule: from the cell to the blood, from the blood to the lungs, and eventually out into the atmosphere again.

• • • •

CHAPTER 5

WHERE THE ACTION IS

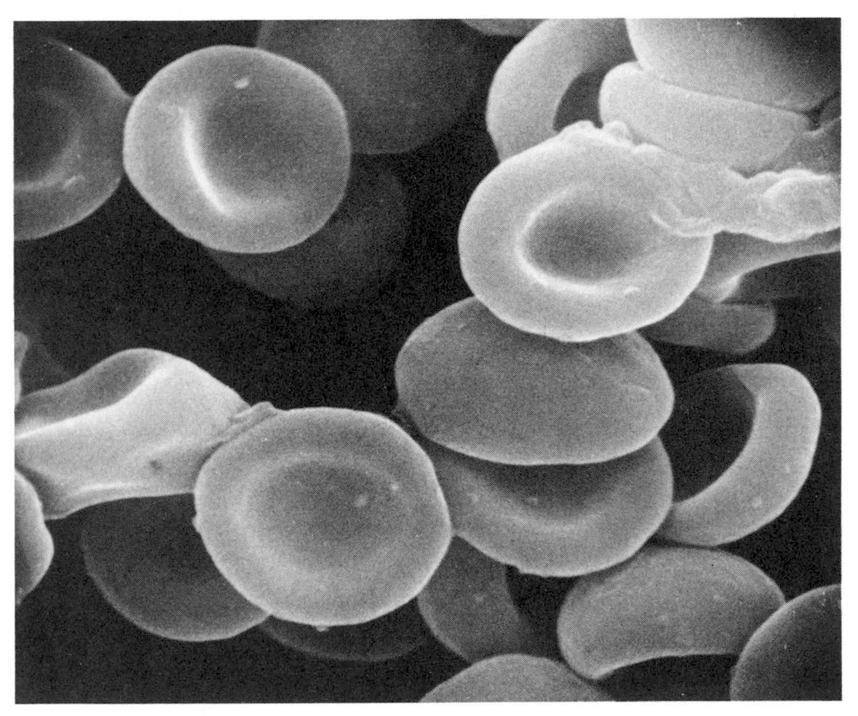

Red blood cells magnified 1,500 times

We already know how air gets into the lungs and how it gets out again. Breathing, however, is only half of the process of respiration. To understand the rest of what happens, we will follow a single molecule of oxygen on its "inner journey": from the lung, where it has been carried by inhalation, to one of the body's cells, where the oxygen will be used.

Oxygen molecules are carried in the blood by *red blood cells.*

must get out of the alveolus and into a blood vessel. Every alveolus is surrounded by the tiny blood vessels called *capillaries.*

Oxygen is able to move from the alveolus to a capillary for two reasons. First, the membrane that the oxygen must cross on its way to the capillary is *permeable* to oxygen. That is, oxygen can pass through the membrane.

The second reason why oxygen can move from the alveolus to a capillary is that there are fewer oxygen molecules in the capillary than there are in the alveolus. That is, the *concentration* of oxygen is lower in the capillary. And it is a natural tendency of gases (materials that can flow in all directions) to move from places where they are more highly concentrated to places where they are less concentrated. Therefore, following this natural tendency, an oxygen molecule will pass *from* the alveolus, where the oxygen concentration is high, through the permeable wall of the alveolus and *into* the capillary, where the oxygen concentration is lower.

After the molecule has passed through the alveolar membrane, it is in the blood vessel. But it has not yet attached itself to its carrier, the red blood cell. Five percent of the oxygen carried in the blood is not attached to red cells; instead it is dissolved in *plasma,* the colorless fluid that remains after red cells are filtered out of the blood. For most oxygen molecules, however, the next step after their passage through the alveolar membrane and into the capillary is to become attached to a *hemoglobin* molecule.

Hemoglobin is the material in red blood cells that "grabs" and holds onto oxygen molecules while the red blood cells travel around the body. As is also true for its passage through the alveolar membrane, oxygen diffuses into red blood cells by osmosis; once there, it combines chemically with hemoglobin to form a new molecule: *oxyhemoglobin.*

Hemoglobin enormously increases the oxygen-carrying capacity of the blood. If it were not for the oxygen-carrying capability of hemoglobin—that is, if oxygen were only dissolved in the plasma of the blood—the heart would have to pump about 130 liters of blood per minute to deliver enough oxygen to the cells. (A liter is a unit of fluid measurement that equals about four standard measuring cups.) However, because blood containing hemoglobin can carry 26 times as much oxygen as could plasma

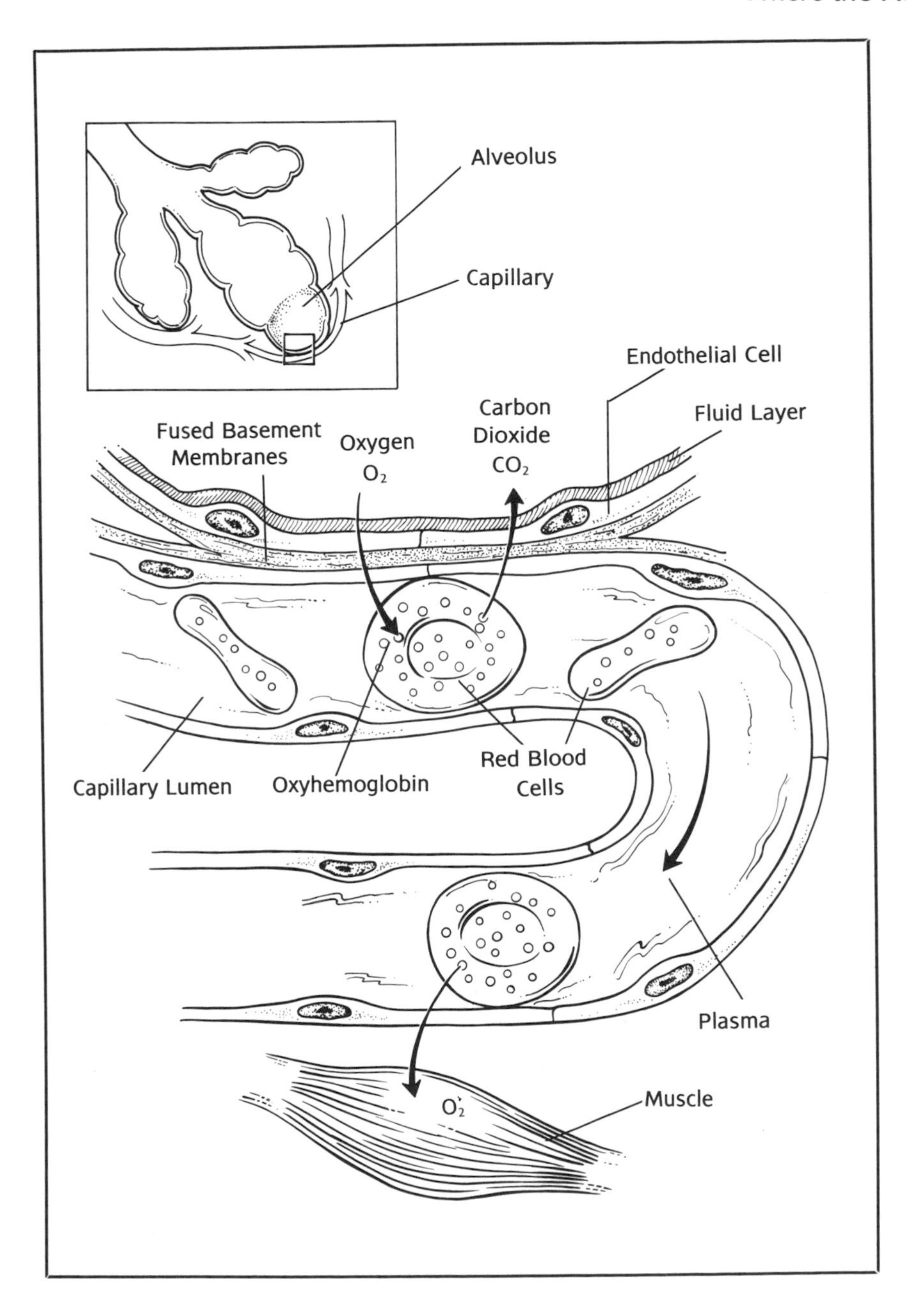

Figure 5: The Pathway of an Oxygen Molecule. *Oxygen diffuses from the alveolar membrane into a capillary, where it is picked up by a hemoglobin molecule, transported to a group of cells, and released.*

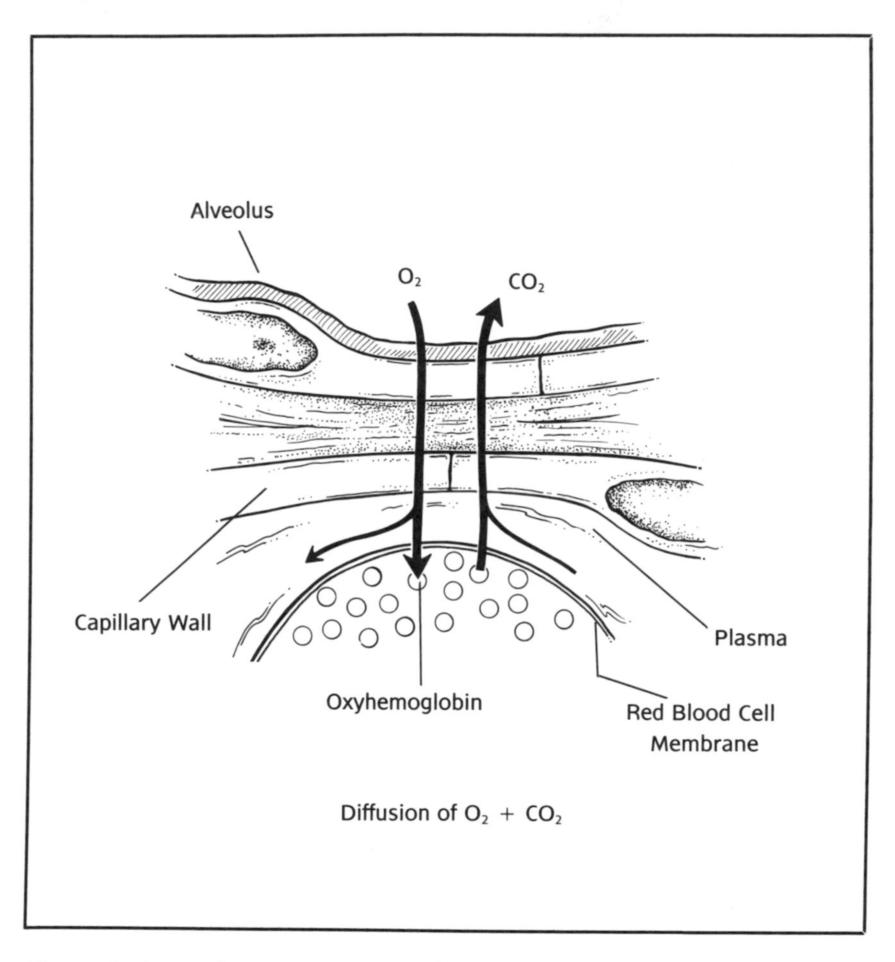

Figure 6: Osmosis. *Oxygen passes from the alveolar membrane to a capillary by osmosis. In this process, a molecule moves from an area where there is a great deal of oxygen to an area where there is little.*

But before an oxygen molecule can ride in a red blood cell, it by itself, the heart of a human adult only has to pump about 5 liters of blood per minute to meet the body's demand for oxygen.

After the oxygen has passed into the blood and become attached to the hemoglobin in a red blood cell, it enters into the next step of respiration. The oxygen-rich blood is pumped out by the heart to the cells of the body; our oxygen-loaded red blood cell travels in the bloodstream until it reaches a group of cells.

There the oxygen detaches itself from the hemoglobin in the red blood cell.

One might wonder why the hemoglobin, so anxious to grab hold of the oxygen molecule as it entered the bloodstream, would let go of the molecule now. The answer is that hemoglobin only grabs and holds oxygen molecules under some conditions: the conditions that exist in oxygen-poor blood near the lung's alveoli. Besides this, the chemical composition and temperature of the blood in the region of the alveoli make hemoglobin bind to and hold oxygen even more firmly.

But when blood reaches the body cells, conditions are different. The oxygen content of a cell is measured in millimeters of mercury—the amount of pressure the oxygen is exerting in the cell. Because this oxygen pressure, or *oxygen tension,* is usually only 40 millimeters of mercury in a body cell, whereas the oxygen tension of the red blood cell is approximately 60 millimeters of mercury, the hemoglobin easily releases its oxygen load, giving up its oxygen to the body cell.

Once again, other factors, such as temperature and chemical composition, influence the readiness of the hemoglobin to release its oxygen. These factors are important safeguards, because under some conditions the cells' requirement for oxygen changes. If the body's temperature is elevated, for example, cells use and require more oxygen—and accordingly, hemoglobin releases more.

There are some conditions under which hemoglobin is unable to release oxygen. You can see the effects of this in yourself: When your hands are very cold, they get red. This is because the hemoglobin in their blood vessels is too cold to give up oxygen. Therefore, blood cells in the vessels stay oxygen-rich, and the bright red, oxygen-rich hemoglobin makes your hands red.

Once the oxygen molecule has been released from the red blood cell and diffused into the body cell, it is used in the body cell's metabolism. Metabolism is an extremely complicated process. An enormous number of chemical reactions must occur in cells to transform the energy held in food molecules—fats, sugars, and proteins—into energy the body can use.

In its simplest terms, however, metabolism is the process in which oxygen enters into a reaction with chemicals already present in a cell—and which originally came from food. This chemical reaction breaks some of the bonds that hold these molecules together. When these bonds are broken, they release energy. Two main by-products of the energy-releasing chemical reaction are water and carbon dioxide.

Our oxygen molecule has now completed its trip, traveling in air into the lungs, from the lungs to the blood, and from the blood to a body cell. In the cell, it has been used in metabolism (energy production). Once this has been accomplished, the substance that is the major waste gas produced by metabolism, carbon dioxide, must be excreted.

The Excretion of Carbon Dioxide

Just as oxygen diffuses from the lungs into capillaries passing through the lungs, so does carbon dioxide diffuse from the body's cells into capillaries near the cells. It does so because there is more carbon dioxide in the body cell, and therefore a greater carbon dioxide pressure or tension, than in the blood. Once carbon dioxide molecules reach the blood, they are carried back toward the lungs in two ways: Some carbon dioxide is dissolved in the plasma, while most enters the red blood cells.

In the red blood cell, some carbon dioxide is dissolved in the cell's water, some is taken up by the hemoglobin, and the remainder, most of the carbon dioxide inside the red blood cell, combines chemically with water molecules to form *carbonic acid.* The chemical formula for a carbonic acid molecule is written H_2CO_3. When the red blood cell reaches the capillaries surrounding the alveoli in the lungs, the carbonic acid molecule is *dehydrated*—a water molecule comes out of it—leaving just a molecule of carbon dioxide.

Once again, because there is more carbon dioxide in the blood than in the alveolus of the lung, the carbon dioxide molecule diffuses from an area of greater concentration—the red blood cell—to an area of lesser concentration—the alveolus. From the alveolus, the carbon dioxide is excreted from the body by exhalation.

The precise chemical details of oxygen transport, carbon dioxide transport, and cell metabolism are much more complex than we have described here. For now, however, it is important to keep two things in mind.

First, the events of respiration in the body do not happen separately. Instead, they are all happening simultaneously. A red blood cell in the lung, for example, takes up oxygen at the very same moment as it gives off carbon dioxide—and this "moment" lasts for less than a second, the length of time a single red blood cell remains in the capillary of the lung.

Second, the respiratory system does not work in isolation. Rather, it operates in concert with the other systems of the body. Blood, for example, could not carry its vital loads around the body if the heart did not pump blood through the blood vessels; in other words, the respiratory system could not work without the circulatory system.

Furthermore, when necessary, the two systems will compensate to some degree for one another's failings. If the lungs are failing or malfunctioning, the heart works harder in an attempt to make up for this deficiency. If the heart is failing, the lungs work harder, attempting to take in more oxygen and eliminate more carbon dioxide by way of more rapid respiration. This is why heart disease may cause a person to feel short of breath, while lung disease can cause a rapid heartbeat.

The other systems of the body also work in concert with one another and with the respiratory and circulatory systems. Carbonic acid, for example, tends to increase the acid content of the entire body, and the body may give off excess acid by way of the kidneys. So if the lungs do not work well and fail to give off enough carbon dioxide, the body will sense the presence of the extra acid and cause the kidneys to excrete it.

Conversely, if the kidneys do not work well and fail to excrete their quota of acid, the body will attempt to give off more carbon dioxide by breathing more rapidly to decrease its acid load. In short, although each system of the body has its own special chores, the different systems do not work in isolation. Instead, they react and respond in complex, interrelated ways, both to one another and to the demands of the body as a whole.

When one of the body's systems becomes unable to do its work or to cooperate normally with the other systems, we say it is diseased. And because the respiratory system's work supports the body's very life, diseases of the respiratory system may be extremely serious. On the other hand, some diseases of the respiratory system, while unpleasant and disruptive, do not usually threaten life. In the next chapter we will see what can go wrong with the respiratory system and examine some of the ways in which physicians help people who are suffering from respiratory difficulties.

• • • •

CHAPTER 6

WHAT CAN GO WRONG?

Perhaps the best known, most widely experienced respiratory difficulty is the common cold. Colds are caused by a number of viruses: rhinoviruses (which cause about 40% of colds), coronaviruses (which cause about 20%), adenoviruses (responsible for about 10%), and enteroviruses (which cause about 10% and are often responsible for "summer colds"). Influenza viruses—the "flu bugs"—and RSV (respiratory syncytial virus) cause most other colds.

Whatever their origin, colds make cells in the nose, throat, and lungs swell, become inflamed, and produce excess mucus. Most young people have experienced symptoms of a cold: chills, fever, sore throat, sneezing, a runny or stuffy nose, and a cough. Students may easily catch colds from one another in school, because cold viruses are spread by coughing and sneezing. A person living in a major city catches, on the average, about three colds each year.

At present there is no medication that will kill cold viruses in the body. Instead, the treatment for colds is symptomatic—its primary purpose is to make the patient feel better. Some people take aspirin for muscle aches that occur with a cold, while others prefer over-the-counter cold medicines, which can lessen the cough and runny nose of a cold.

However, it is best to use over-the-counter medications with caution, and only when absolutely necessary. Many such medications have unpleasant and unwanted side effects, such as drowsiness, an increased heart rate, and lightheadedness. Furthermore, in "drying up" the extra mucus the body is secreting, these preparations may also thicken it. Thickened mucus gives bacteria a place in which to grow, and so may allow another, more serious infection to take hold.

Aspirin may also be an unwise remedy, because cold viruses are killed by higher-than-normal body temperatures, which aspirin reduces. The best treatment for a cold is a day or two of bed rest, not only because cold sufferers feel ill but also because staying in bed keeps the infection from spreading to others, and a high fluid intake—water or orange juice, for example. Although colds can be irritating, they do have one good point: Eventually, they go away by themselves. They may also help the body protect itself against more serious diseases: A study conducted by Professor Kurt S. Zänker at the University of Witten–Herdicke in West Germany on cancer patients showed that people who suffer less than one cold every year are six times more likely to develop cancer than those who catch one or more colds each year, probably because colds "rev up" the body's immune system, which is responsible for attacking cancer cells as well.

Asthma

Another respiratory difficulty that affects both many young people and adults is asthma. About 1% of the population suffers from asthma; among children under 15, the rate is between 5 and 15%.

Asthma occurs in "attacks" that may come on slowly or all at once, and the main symptom is always shortness of breath. The victim's lungs feel tight, as if he or she were suffocating. All of the victim's attention and energy must be devoted to getting each breath. The air that does manage to get in makes a whistling, "wheezing" sound as it passes through the tightened air passages. An asthma attack is often frightening, exhausting, and sometimes dangerous, because although most attacks pass with treatment or by themselves, a severe asthma attack that does not respond to treatment can cause death. About 5,000 people die of asthma each year in the United States.

During an asthma attack, the smooth muscle around the airways in the lungs (the bronchi and bronchioles) constricts, squeezing the airways. This squeezed condition is called *bronchospasm*. Meanwhile, the membranes inside the airways may swell, and there may be excess mucus production. All these factors, and especially smooth-muscle constriction, make the airways so narrow that air can barely pass through them.

Asthma may be *extrinsic*, caused by an allergy or airway-irritating infection, or *intrinsic*, caused by factors within the body that may remain unidentified. Anxiety and stress may also contribute to the frequency and severity of asthma attacks.

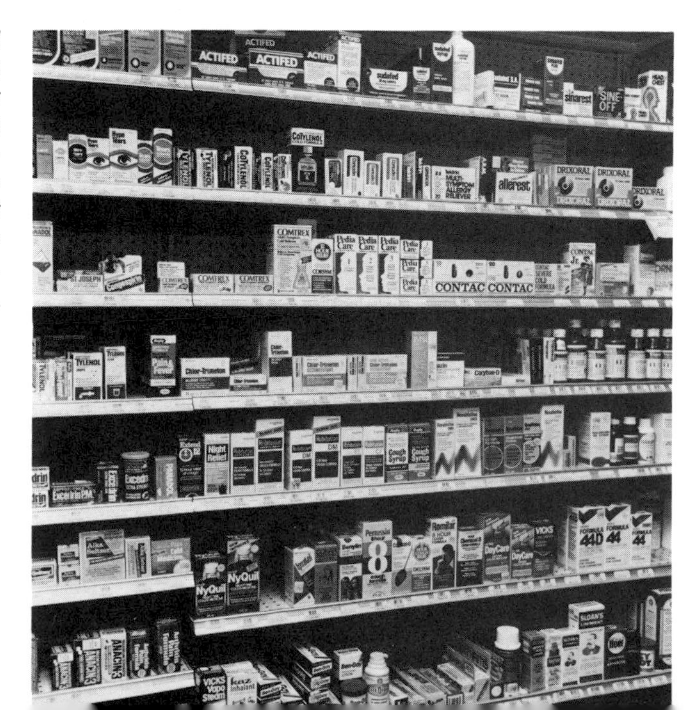

Over-the-counter cold and allergy medications may provide temporary relief but can also have many unwanted side effects, including drowsiness, increased heart rate, and light-headedness.

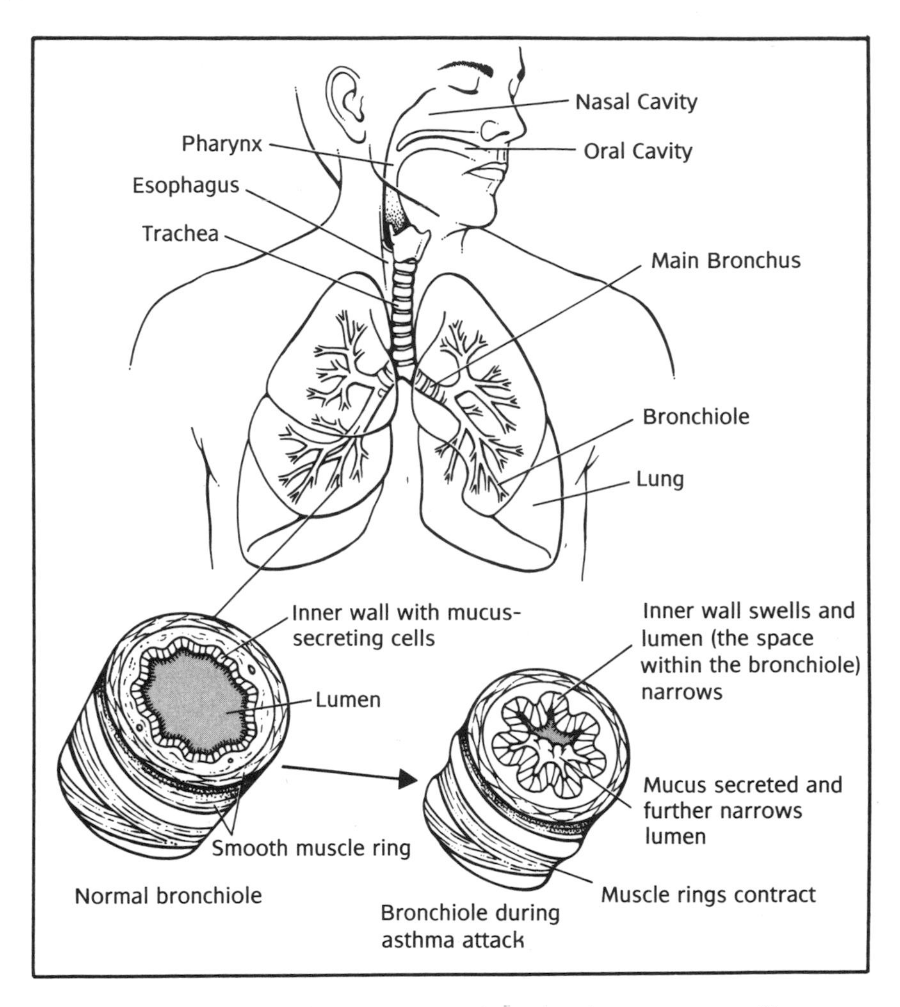

***Figure 7: Asthma Attack.** A diagram of the respiratory system illustrates the physical changes that take place in the bronchioles during an asthma attack.*

The general treatment of asthma may include desensitization treatment for allergies that trigger asthma attacks. This entails the introduction into the patient's body, in gradually increased, controlled amounts, of the material that causes the allergy. The purpose of this is to allow the body to "get used to"—or build up a tolerance for—the offending substance. Other patients are treated with steroids, such as prednisone, in order to control the body's reaction to allergens. Antibiotic drugs for respiratory infections, the avoidance of attack-triggering irritants such as dust or animal hairs, and counseling to reduce the anxiety component of the disease may also be part of asthma treatment.

Some medical professionals recommend deep, diaphragmatic breathing, or learning to breathe from the diaphragm, to help control the occurrence of asthma attacks. Other approaches, such as hypnosis, meditation, and acupuncture are also sometimes used to control asthma.

To stop an acute attack of asthma, the patient can inhale a medicated mist that relaxes smooth muscles around the affected airways. This medicine is called a *bronchodilator* (airway widener). It may be of the over-the-counter type, such as Primatene mist, or it may be a prescription drug. Isoetharine (Bronkosol), metaproterenol (Alupent), and albuterol (Ventolin) are among the prescription drugs used to relieve acute attacks of asthma. Disodium cromoglyate (Intal or Cromolyn Sodium) may prevent attacks when inhaled regularly—although it does not stop an attack once one has begun.

If an asthma attack is severe, the patient may be forced to enter the hospital for oxygen, observation, and intravenous (given directly through the vein) asthma medication. During certain parts of the year, when the weather is particularly humid or the pollen count unusually high, it is not unusual to find several persons with asthma in the emergency room of a local hospital.

Although most people with asthma carry a small inhaler containing bronchodilator medication in a pocket or purse, asthma medicine, whether over-the-counter or prescription, has strong side effects, particularly on the heart. So perhaps the most important thing for a person with asthma to remember is: Don't overuse the "pocket inhaler." If you use it and do not get the relief you usually get, do not simply use it until you do. Overuse of asthma medicine, as with any drug, will build up a tolerance for the drug that will make it necessary to take ever-increasing amounts to achieve the desired effect. Instead of overusing the medicine, visit a physician or go to the emergency room of your local hospital.

Although asthma can be a frightening and sometimes dangerous disease, in the vast majority of cases it can be controlled. Medication, breathing techniques, regular exercise, and the removal of allergens from the home can help people with asthma to lead healthy, normal lives.

Childhood Asthma

Nearly 8 million children in the United States suffer from asthma. Although some do outgrow the disease by building up an immunity, the number of deaths from asthma has risen 23% since 1980. Tragically, many of these victims are children. This trend is attributable to an increase in environmental irritants and pollutants and to inadequate medical care. Many of the children receive too little care too late or are simply unable to cope with the disease and let themselves die instead of seeking help for an attack.

Asthma attacks occur when the body's airways become blocked, causing wheezing or breathlessness. This obstruction can be caused by mucus, swollen membranes, or a tightening of the muscles in the airways, and it is most often treated with medication. Most physicians believe that asthma can be controlled so that people, especially children, can learn to anticipate and avoid irritants or aggravating physical changes that can bring on an attack, thus giving them some control over the disease.

Children suffering from asthma should learn to understand what their disease is, how it is brought on, and what they can do to avoid, or cope with, an attack. Many asthma specialists suggest breathing techniques that teach the asthmatic to fill and empty the lungs completely and exercises such as blowing a piece of paper or Ping-Pong ball across the floor to build up endurance. Other physicians believe that relaxation techniques or self-hypnosis enable some young patients to deal with their attacks calmly when they occur and to control the emotional responses that can also trigger an attack.

One thing all physicians agree on is that the parents of asthmatic children should make sure their child takes his or her medicine faithfully and receives prompt medical attention when necessary. With this combined family and medical support, experts believe, children can learn to cope with asthma and to develop the healthy outlook necessary to fight the disease and live a normal life.

Bronchitis

Another fairly common respiratory disease is bronchitis. As its name implies, bronchitis is an inflammation of the membranes lining the bronchi—the airways in the lungs. Caused by bacteria such as *Streptococcus, Hemophilus,* and others, bronchitis often occurs in people who are already ill with a viral infection, such as a cold, the flu, or measles. Acute bronchitis causes a fever, a sore throat, and a cough that produces thick mucus. It usually improves by itself or with antibiotic treatment; the patient commonly feels well again within a few days, but may have a cough for several weeks.

In chronic bronchitis, the cough either does not go away or returns frequently. The main symptom of this disease is a persistent cough that produces mucus. The root cause of chronic bronchitis is usually cigarette smoking, air pollution, or a long history of inhaling irritating materials such as dust or chemical fumes at work. Lungs damaged by these materials are susceptible to infections, which can do even more damage. Year after year, the cough of chronic bronchitis gets worse and infections are more frequent.

The best treatment for chronic bronchitis is to eliminate sources of lung irritation: to stop smoking, avoid dust and chemical fumes, and avoid catching colds or other infections as much as possible.

Pneumonia

So far, the respiratory diseases we have discussed will either go away by themselves or can in most cases be treated fairly easily. A more severe disease of the respiratory system, which can permanently damage the lungs and may also be quite difficult to cure, is pneumonia.

Pneumonia is an acute infection, not just of the airways but of the lung tissue itself. It may be caused by many different organisms, including viruses, bacteria, fungi, and other kinds of germs.

Common bacterial causes of pneumonia include *Staphylococcus, Streptococcus,* (of which the pneumococcus *Streptococcus pneumonia* is the most common cause of the disease) and *Klebsiella*. One-fourth of all pneumonias are caused by a virus; among these, the influenza virus is the most common. Other organisms that cause pneumonia include mycoplasmas, which are not classified as bacteria or viruses but are the smallest free-living agents of disease in humans.

After a surgical operation, staying in bed too long and failing to cough up mucus from the lungs can allow pneumonia to develop (usually a fungal, bacterial, or viral pneumonia), as will a tumor that obstructs the airways so that mucus cannot be cleared. A few pneumonias are not caused by germs at all: Accidentally inhaling a caustic liquid or a gas such as chlorine will cause a chemical pneumonia.

Fever, chills, a cough, chest pain, body aches, shortness of breath, a rapid heartbeat, blueness of the lips (because the body is not getting enough oxygen), and the general feeling of being very ill are some of the symptoms of pneumonia.

The treatment for pneumonia depends on the cause. Antibiotic drugs are almost always effective against bacteria and mycoplasmas. Against virus-caused pneumonias, there are no effective antibiotics; the treatment for these diseases consists of support-

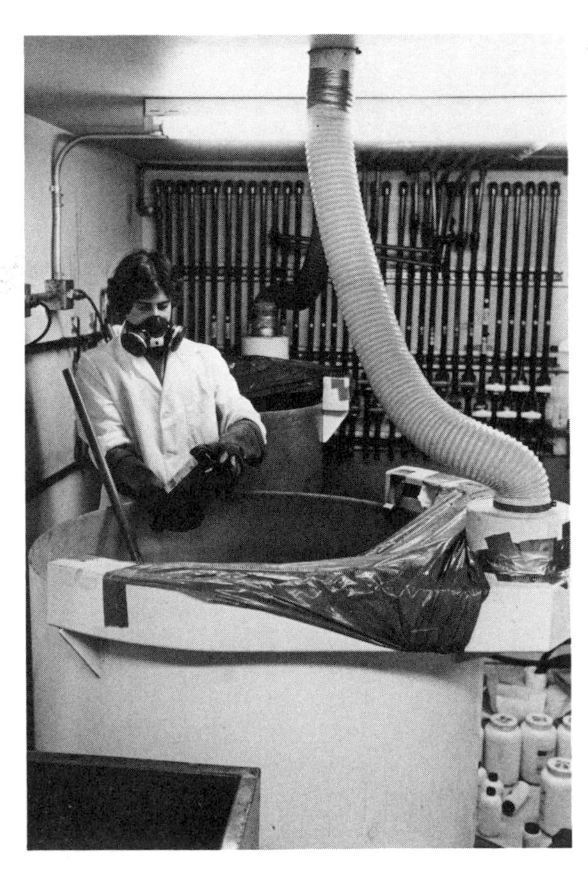

A worker at a film lab wears a protective mask while handling chemicals. Protective masks can filter out many harmful pollutants and particles that could damage the respiratory system.

ing the patient with oxygen, fluids, nutrition, and pain medications until the disease has run its course.

The prognosis in cases of pneumonia also varies. Some pneumonias, especially in older people and those weakened by other diseases, are fatal. But the average healthy young person or adult who develops pneumonia can most likely be cured by antibiotics and will recover after an illness of several weeks. But even then it is important for the person to eat well, get plenty of rest, and in general continue to follow the doctor's advice. Otherwise a relapse (another bout of pneumonia) can occur.

Cystic Fibrosis

Another serious respiratory disease affecting young people is cystic fibrosis. A genetic disease, it is inherited, being caused by genes that are transmitted to the affected individual by his or her parents.

Cystic fibrosis affects the secretions of the *exocrine glands*—those producing sweat, mucus, saliva, and digestive juices. In the disease, these glands produce abnormally thick secretions—so thick they can plug up organs such as the pancreas, the liver, and the lungs. Because the airways in the lungs become plugged with these mucus secretions, air cannot easily pass through them. Also, plugged lungs are especially apt to get infected.

The disease occurs in 1 out of every 1,500 Caucasian (white) infants who are born alive (some very severely affected infants die before birth). It rarely occurs in black infants and almost never in Asians.

The definitive test for cystic fibrosis is the sweat test. In this test sweat is collected from the skin and analyzed. A high electrolyte (salt) content in the sweat indicates that the person has the disease. Patients with cystic fibrosis are often very thin because the disease affects their digestion, and they get frequent colds and pneumonias. They have a chronic cough that produces very thick, sticky mucus. Their chests may become barrel-shaped as air is trapped behind mucus plugs and they struggle to breathe, and their fingernails become "clubbed" (smooth and rounded).

Cystic fibrosis was at one time always fatal in early childhood. Now, however, although there is still no cure for the disease, increasing numbers of people with cystic fibrosis survive into adolescence and even into adulthood. Vitamins and medicines to aid digestion are one reason for this, but another reason is effective treatments for the respiratory aspect of the disease. These are as follows:

1. Postural drainage, in which the patient lies head down several times each day while someone claps him or her on the chest and back. This loosens mucus, which may then be more easily coughed up.
2. Medications that are inhaled in the form of a mist. These include mucolytic agents (to dissolve mucus) and broncho-dilating drugs (to widen the airways).
3. Antibiotics, both systemic (in the form of injections or pills) and inhaled as mists.

Together, these treatments are helping more and more persons with cystic fibrosis to survive and thrive, while research continues daily to find more and better ways of helping them lead longer, healthier lives.

Other Respiratory Diseases

A condition of the respiratory system that may arise suddenly in young people is spontaneous pneumothorax. In it, a sudden, small break in the pleura, the membrane covering the lung, lets air leak into the pleural space (the space between the lung and chest wall). Spontaneous pneumothorax occurs most commonly in males between the ages of 15 and 35.

The most common cause of spontaneous pneumothorax is a burst bleb—a small blister or spot in the pleura that breaks when it becomes overinflated and weakened, like a balloon blown up too much. At times, the opening that results from this rupture lets so much air leak into the pleural space that it presses on the lung, causing it to partially collapse.

The symptoms of a spontaneous pneumothorax are a sudden, sharp chest pain and shortness of breath with no obvious cause, although sometimes there may be only a dull aching. No previous sign of ill health is generally evident. The condition is treated by inserting a tube through the chest wall to drain out the air that has leaked in and surgery to remove the damaged area of the lung and pleura, so that it does not break again.

A whole range of respiratory diseases may begin in young

adulthood, yet produce no symptoms until middle age or later. These are the diseases caused by cigarette smoking. One major disease of smokers is emphysema.

Together, chronic bronchitis and emphysema are known as chronic obstructive pulmonary disease, or COPD. About 4% of the adult population of the United States has some form of this disease. Heredity apparently plays some role in its development; about 5% of people in the United States are deficient in a lung enzyme called alpha-antitrypsin, making them vulnerable to emphysema even if they do not smoke. But the major factor responsible for COPD is cigarette smoking. In some studies of emphysema, more than 90% of the people who have the disease either are or have been heavy smokers.

Over time, cigarette smoke cripples the lungs' defense system. It is estimated that 83% of all lung cancers are smoking related.

In emphysema, the lungs produce large amounts of excess mucus and the alveoli get "baggy," losing their springiness, or elasticity. As it becomes more and more difficult for the body to exhale, air becomes trapped in the lungs, overexpanding them. Eventually, their walls disintegrate. Now the lungs cannot efficiently move air at all, much less pass oxygen and carbon dioxide efficiently into and out of the blood. As a result the heart pumps harder, trying to make up for the lungs' problems. The outcome is heart damage, compounding the pulmonary difficulty.

The earliest sign of emphysema is a chronic cough. Later,

Congressman Jack Mullendore speaks in favor of a bill to limit smoking in public buildings in 1986. Mullendore, a smoker for many years, was forced to use a portable oxygen tank after contracting emphysema.

shortness of breath develops and progresses until the patient is short of breath even while at rest. Imagine being short of breath all the time, to the point of panic; this is what the end stages of emphysema feel like.

Eventually, emphysema causes death. There is no cure for the disease and no way to repair lungs injured by it. But its progress can be halted if the patient stops smoking. If that is accomplished, the lungs will repair themselves to some extent.

In addition, medical treatment can provide some relief for the symptoms of emphysema, with antibiotics being used to treat infection, postural drainage and inhaled medications to remove excess mucus, and oxygen treatment to supply what the lungs can no longer obtain from ordinary air. Another major respiratory disease that has been scientifically linked to cigarette smoking is lung cancer. In this disease a cancerous tumor grows in the tissue of the lung, most often in one of the bronchi. As it grows, the tumor blocks an increasing number of airways and destroys ever more alveoli, preventing normal respiration. It may also invade blood vessels, the pleura covering the lung, and the chest wall, and spread to other parts of the body as well.

In 1987, 150,000 new cases of lung cancer were diagnosed. The survival rate for patients with this disease remained low, and only 13% were living 5 years after the diagnosis was made. Once a disease more common in men, lung cancer is now the number one cause of cancer deaths among women.

Smoking causes an estimated 83% of all lung cancers. Those persons whose jobs cause them to breathe polluted air, especially in radioactive areas such as uranium mines and areas contaminated with asbestos (an insulation material), also have higher than normal rates of lung cancer.

The best way to prevent lung cancer is not to smoke and not to breathe polluted air. Prompt attention to the signs and symptoms of lung cancer, such as a new or unusual kind of cough, spitting up blood, chronic chest pain, or unexplained weight loss, increases the chances of surviving the disease.

Lung cancer is almost never seen in young people. But by avoiding habits and situations that cause the disease, young people can decrease their chances of developing lung cancer when they get older.

By contrast, a potentially fatal respiratory condition that can occur at any age is an acute obstruction, or choking: the accidental inhaling of food or a solid object into the airway. For example, infants who put beads or small toys into their mouths may inhale them, and anyone may inhale a poorly chewed piece of food. The inhaling of an object into the trachea—the body's only route for taking air into the lungs—is a true airway emergency and may cause death.

The causes of acute airway obstruction are varied, but one common cause is talking and laughing while at the same time trying to chew food. People who suffer airway obstruction in restaurants often look as if they are having a heart attack, when in fact they have probably inhaled a piece of food. This situation is so common that it is known as a "café coronary."

The main symptom of acute airway obstruction is the sudden inability to breathe or speak. If you see someone who appears to be having this difficulty, ask: "Can you speak?" If the person cannot, his or her airway is probably blocked by a foreign object. Only three minutes remain before the person suffers brain damage from lack of oxygen.

A cross section, rear aspect, of a pair of healthy lungs. This photo clearly shows the healthy lung tissue and the passages of the bronchi. The heart is shown in place, bottom, left.

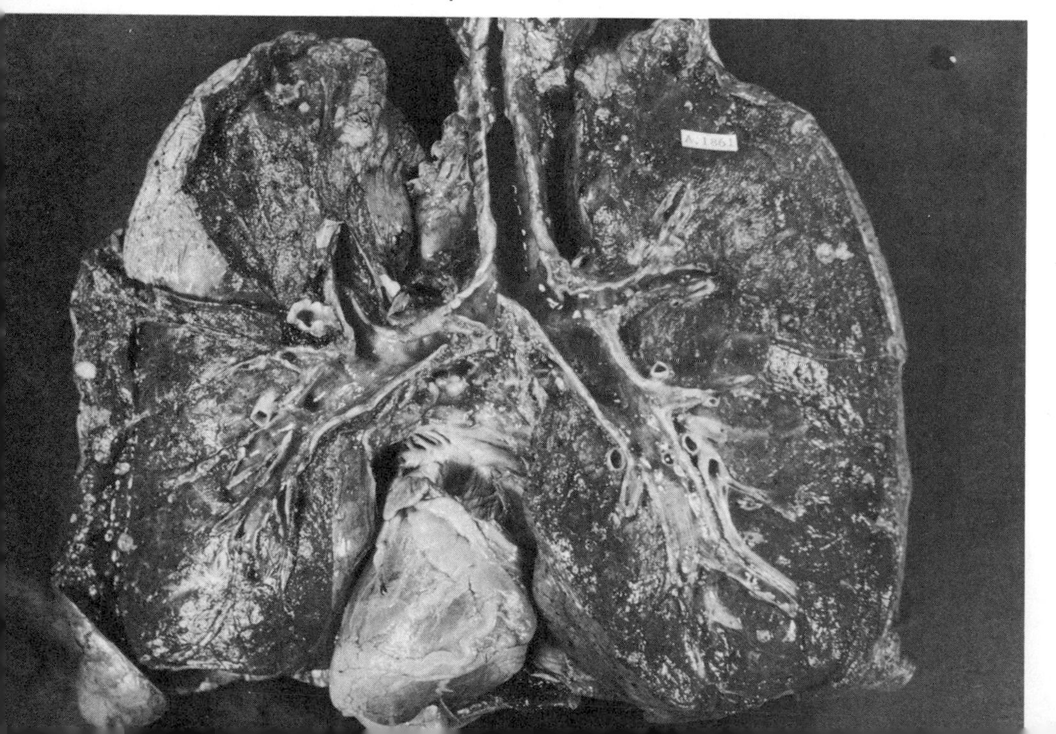

The treatment in such an emergency has several steps: (1) Try to remove the offending material from the victim's airway by bending the person forward and striking a sharp blow to the middle of the person's back; (2) If this does not dislodge the food, then grasp the choking person firmly around the midsection, clasp your hands together, and bring them up firmly at a point just below the victim's breastbone. Alternate and repeat these two steps, if necessary; and (3) Call an ambulance or have someone else call one while you stay with the victim. For the treatment of an emergency airway obstruction that is not relieved at once, you need to get trained medical help immediately.

Some respiratory diseases, such as asthma, cystic fibrosis, and the common cold, can afflict people while they are young, but others, such as chronic obstructive lung disease and lung cancer, do not appear until later in life. Tuberculosis (a disease caused by bacteria that often settles in and breaks down the lungs), once thought to have been wiped out by vaccinations, is on the rise again. The diseases of late adulthood are of concern to young people as well, because many habits or practices that cause these diseases are formed early in life. In this chapter, we have ex-

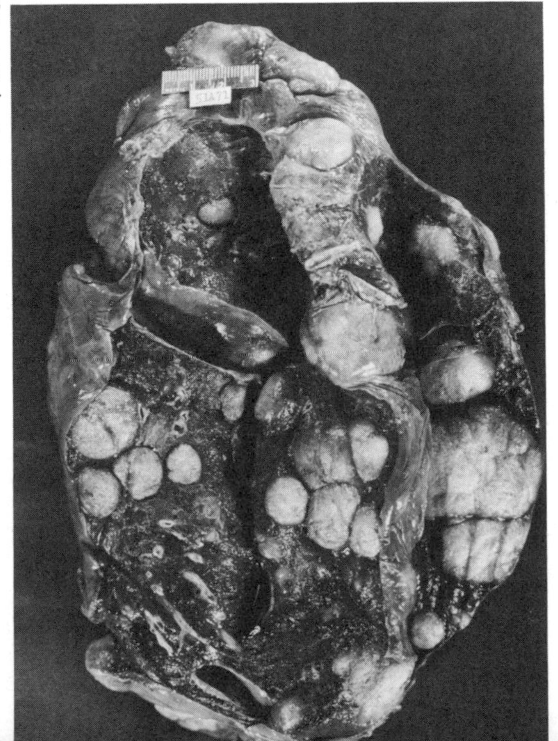

A single lung riddled with cancerous tumors. Refraining from smoking and avoiding polluted air decrease the risk of developing lung cancer.

amined just a few of the difficulties that can affect a person's respiratory system.

In the next chapter we will see how the respiratory system defends itself against injury and disease and examine some common threats to the respiratory system, along with methods of avoiding them. We will also name some public and private health associations that are working toward better breathing, not only for young people but for everyone.

• • • •

CHAPTER 7

GUARDING THE BREATH OF LIFE

Elaborate defenses guard the respiratory system from disease and injury. In the nose, hair filters out large foreign particles, while the mucous membranes of the upper respiratory system warm and humidify incoming air. Mucus in the nose also catches dirt and some bacteria. By the time it reaches the trachea, inhaled air is warm, moist, and cleansed of particles larger than 10 microns in diameter. (A micron is one-thousandth of a millimeter; two and a half millimeters equal one inch.)

Irritating particles in the nose may trigger a sneeze, the body's reflex action to expel such irritants, by stimulating nerve endings in the mucous membranes of the nasopharynx. The nerve impulses that cause sneezes can be "turned off" by pressing hard with a finger under the nose, because pressure on the nerves in this location briefly blocks these impulses.

The epiglottis performs its protective function by acting as a lid on the larynx, but when nearby areas are irritated by foreign material, the larynx itself may constrict in a condition called *laryngospasm,* which prevents irritants from entering the trachea.

Experiments have shown that nonirritating substances do not cause the larynx to close, and they may therefore be inhaled past it. If, however, the epiglottis is paralyzed by injury or disease, or if a person is unconscious, even irritating substances may enter the airways. Drug or alcohol overdosage often causes this, because the victim's stomach tries to rid itself of drugs or alcohol by vomiting. But the unconscious victim does not "gag" and therefore spit up the vomited material, and the gastric contents instead flow into the unprotected airways, with potentially fatal results.

Even when the upper respiratory system's defenses work, some dust, bacteria, and viruses are able to pass into the lungs and bronchi, but the lower parts of the system have their own defenses against these. Ninety percent of particles larger than two microns in diameter are caught in mucus that is moved upward to the pharynx by the whipping action of the cilia.

About 250 cilia, each about a half micron long and a quarter of a micron in diameter, grow from each of the special epithelial cells lining the larger bronchi. Between the epithelial cells are the *goblet cells* that produce almost half a cup of mucus every 24 hours.

Beating about 1,000 to 1,500 times per minute, the cilia move the mucous layer and the foreign matter in it at the rate of 10 to 20 millimeters per minute—about a mile per week. When the foreign matter and the mucus reach the upper airways, they can be coughed out.

The cough begins in nerve endings in the larynx, trachea, and larger bronchi, when foreign matter or mucus irritates them. The next phase of the cough is a deep breath. Then the glottis closes and the chest and abdominal muscles "squeeze." Finally the glottis opens and the breath caused by the squeezing muscles blasts out, carrying the foreign matter out of the body.

Particles smaller than two microns in diameter may reach very small airways and the alveoli, where some particles are digested by scavenger cells called *macrophages*. Macrophages work so

Figure 8: The Defense System. *An illustration of how the respiratory defense system handles intruders, in this case a dust particle, in the lungs (top) and in the bloodstream (bottom). Shown at right is a magnification of the cilia in the lungs.*

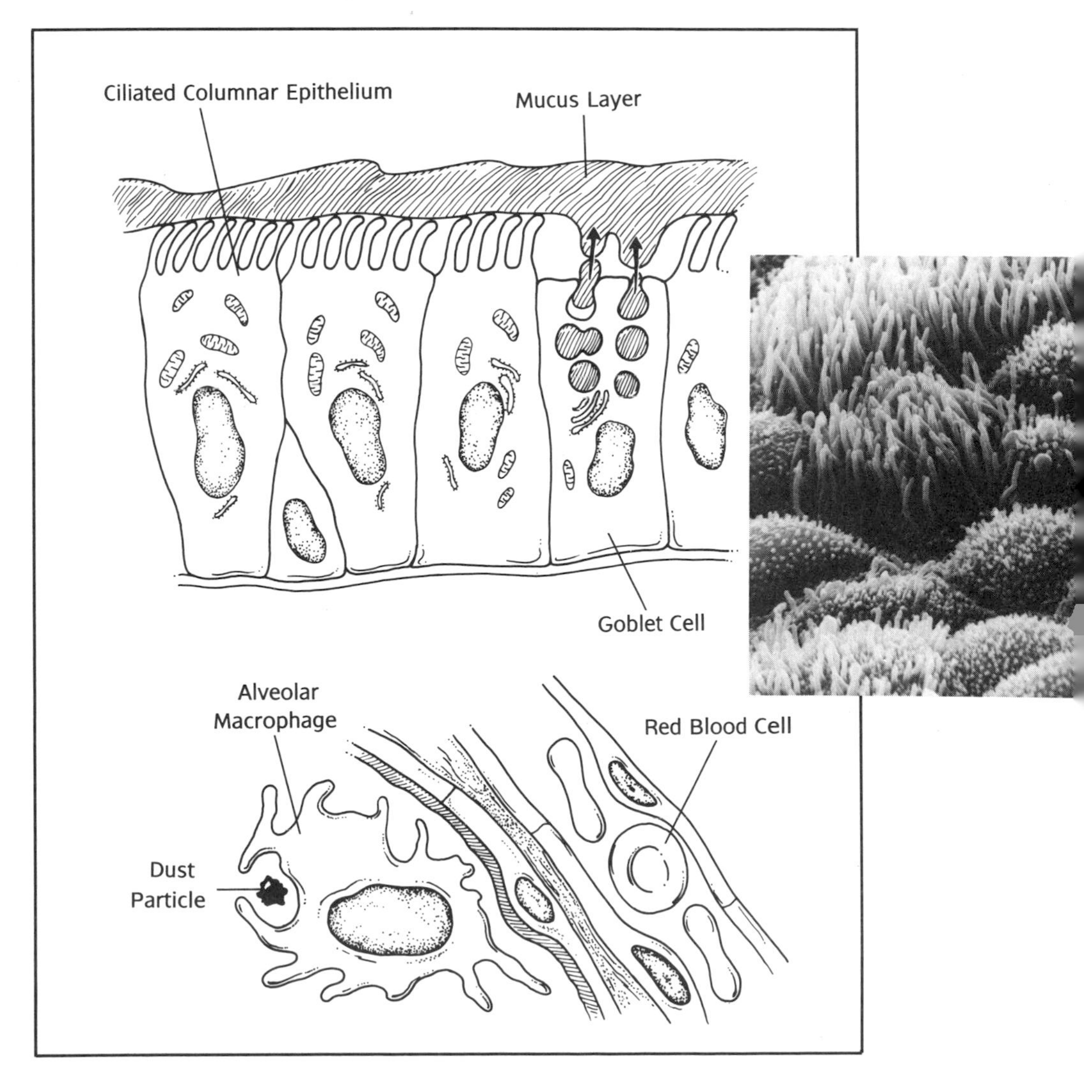

efficiently that even though many bacteria reach the alveoli, the alveoli remain sterile. Nonliving particles such as dust are also taken up by macrophages and moved to the mucus-and-cilia transport system in the larger airways. There are about 600 million macrophages in the lungs of an adult human being.

Smoking: Breaching the Lungs' Defenses

Despite the respiratory system's elaborate defenses, some bacteria, viruses, and other irritants are able to enter the lungs and cause damage. Many lung diseases are the result of such "unauthorized entry." Cigarette smoke is one substance that can breach the lungs' defenses. Many of the particles a burning cigarette gives off are too small to be caught in the mucus of the respiratory tract, and the toxic gases it emits are not kept out at all.

Cigarette smoke causes the bronchial cilia to beat more slowly, crippling the mucus-and-cilia transport system. Thus bacteria can stay in the lung and reproduce—one reason why smokers experience more respiratory infections than do nonsmokers.

Cigarette smoke also stimulates goblet cells to produce extra mucus, which the bronchial cilia, whose action has been slowed, have a hard time moving. This extra mucus gives bacteria a good place in which to multiply and can also plug up the airways. Furthermore, tobacco smoke damages macrophages, which are then unable to dispose of the foreign matter that collects in the mucus and airways. In addition to this, tobacco smoke is able to deposit its own bits of matter—sticky bits of tar that force the lungs to secrete enzymes in an attempt to destroy or negate the effects of the tar. Unfortunately, the enzymes, while neutralizing the irritation caused by the tar, at the same time cause their own damage in the lung. In the long run, these enzymes can destroy lung tissues.

The main gas made by a burning cigarette is carbon monoxide. A carbon monoxide molecule crosses into the blood just as an oxygen molecule can, and once there it attaches itself to the hemoglobin in a red blood cell and hangs on, preventing the hemoglobin from carrying oxygen. So a smoker's blood not only receives less oxygen, but is also kept from carrying much of what it is able to get.

Even secondhand smoke from someone else's cigarette can

cause health difficulties: asthma attacks, for instance. Studies show that children in households where someone smokes get more respiratory infections than children in smoke-free homes. Thus the smoker's last-ditch defense—"I'm only hurting myself"—is not true. Smoking hurts all who come into contact with it, even those who do not themselves smoke, through increased health risks, medical and health-insurance costs, and lowered productivity at work in business and industry.

Smoking causes about 30% of all cancer deaths, as well as contributing to heart disease and many other ailments. The total cost of smoking to the American economy is estimated to be about $65 billion per year, or about $2.17 for every pack of cigarettes sold in the nation.

Environmental Pollution

Some lung damage comes not from things people do actively, such as smoking, but from things done nondeliberately, such as breathing polluted air. Air may be polluted by particles, gases, radioactivity, or a combination of these things.

In a coal mine, for example, the air is often contaminated by coal dust: particles of coal small enough to get into the lungs. Over periods of years, these dust particles build up in miners' lungs, causing "black lung disease," in which a chronic cough and chest pain lead to shortness of breath, severe lung damage, and finally death.

A historic photograph of young coal miners, taken in 1908 by the master photographer Lewis Hine. Over the years, coal dust builds up in a miner's lungs, causing a fatal disease known as "black lung."

Asbestos, a mineral used to make insulation for buildings, causes similar trouble when tiny particles are inhaled by workers in factories that process asbestos, by people who install insulation, and by people in buildings that have this type of insulation. Asbestos causes asbestosis, a respiratory disease caused by the inhalation of asbestos particles, and to cancer. Some studies estimate that 17% of all cancers are linked to asbestos exposure, while smokers exposed to asbestos have a risk of developing lung cancer 60 times higher than unexposed nonsmokers.

Other particles that cause lung disease are cotton fibers (byssinosis), sugar cane dust (bagassosis), fibers from moldy hay (farmer's lung), and iron dust (siderosis). Workers who mine radioactive ores such as uranium or who work in factories where these ores are used may inhale particles of radioactive dust. The radioactivity from the particles (radioactivity is a form of energy) passes through living tissue and damages it, often causing cancer.

Silicon (a mineral that occurs in the dust of mines and in areas where sandblasting, stone grinding, and similar activities take place) causes silicosis, another disease that produces coughing, shortness of breath, chest pain, and eventual death. Until the last half of the 20th century, silicosis was so common that workers in different industries had different names for it. China makers called it potter's asthma, for instance, while among stone grinders the same disorder was known as grinder's rot.

Today silicosis is largely prevented by rules restricting the amount of dust that may be present in workers' air. The National Institute of Occupational Safety and Health and the Labor Department's Occupational Safety Division monitor dust in work areas and can fine employers who violate safety standards. Chemical fumes such as chlorine and gasoline vapors are also monitored.

The workplace is not the only place harboring dangers to the respiratory system. The air we breathe every day is contaminated by factories, incinerators, automobiles, and other sources of pollution. Air pollution was recognized early as a threat to health by the city of Pittsburgh when in 1815 it adopted laws restricting the amount of smoke a chimney owner could put into the air. In 1881, Chicago and Cincinnati adopted laws similar to Pittsburgh's; by 1912, 20 of the 28 American cities with populations of more than 200,000 had smoke-control laws.

Workers with special protective clothing and respirators remove illegally dumped asbestos dust. Inhalation of asbestos, a mineral used in insulation, causes a respiratory disease called asbestosis.

In 1948, in Donora, Pennsylvania, a 5-day air pollution crisis sickened half the town's 14,000 inhabitants and killed 20. In 1952, in London, a similar crisis killed an estimated 4,000. Also in the 1940s, residents of Los Angeles began complaining of a new type of air pollution: smog, produced by the action of sunlight on car exhaust and industrial smoke. In 1953, smog took 200 lives in an early air-pollution crisis in New York City.

In 1955, public demand resulted in the first federal clean-air program. In 1963, the federal Clean Air Act required states to make plans for reducing the six major air pollutants: particles, sulfur and nitrogen oxides, carbon monoxide, hydrocarbons, and photochemical oxidants (chemicals that react when exposed to sunlight).

In 1965, the amended Clean Air Act established controls for motor-vehicle emissions; in 1967 it created a system for national air-pollution control. In 1970 and 1977 states were directed to meet federal air-cleanliness standards. The U.S. Environmental Protection Agency (EPA), charged with putting the Clean Air Act into practice, eliminated lead from most gasoline and tightened emission standards. It also set up 8,000 air-cleanliness monitoring stations across the United States, which continuously record data to track progress in decreasing air pollution.

The Clean Air Act has resulted in measurably cleaner air in dozens of cities, but the EPA has been forced to extend air clean-

Heavy smog cloaks the downtown Los Angeles skyline. Produced by the action of sunlight on car exhaust and industrial smoke, smog was first noticed by residents of Los Angeles in the 1940s.

liness deadlines, first from 1977 to 1982, and then until 1987. In 1987 more than 60 large cities did not meet federal standards, and 12 of the largest cities in America did not have pollution control plans that met the EPA requirements.

Ozone is a toxic form of oxygen given off by engines and manufacturing processes. A pollutant at ground level, it occurs naturally high above the earth in a level of the atmosphere called the stratosphere. Because the ozone layer of the stratosphere filters the sun's rays, preventing many damaging ultraviolet rays from reaching the surface of the earth, the destruction of natural ozone could lead to increased rates of skin cancer, widespread injury to food plants, and eventual destructive changes in the earth's climate. Aerosol cans are major culprits threatening the earth's ozone layer, because the fluorocarbon molecules they contain and spray out chemically combine with ozone molecules, thus removing bits of the ozone layer.

One reason for failure to meet federal air-pollution standards is that doing so costs money. Different pollutants require different methods of removal—including equipment that factories must buy, install, and run. Sulfur dioxide, for example, is made when coal is burned—often in power plants. It is removed by a device known as a "scrubber," in which the dioxide is exposed to limestone and water. Scrubbers remove 90% of the sulfur dioxide that passes through them, but use 5% of a power plant's energy output and make huge amounts of calcium sulfite sludge, a byproduct that must be disposed of.

Methods for removing other pollutants are the cyclone separator, which whirls particulate emissions around like a centrifuge, forcing the particles down to a catch basin; the electrostatic precipitator, which gives particles a charge of static electricity so they will cling to a metal plate; and the baghouse, which is like a huge vacuum cleaner.

All of these machines cost money and reduce a company's profits. Factories complain that they would go out of business if forced to use them. Authorities at the EPA know that if they drive factories from business, the public outcry over lost jobs will create political pressure that could drive the EPA out of existence. It is because of this that in 1984, for example, the EPA was forced to allow 11 states to put 16,000 tons more sulfur dioxide into the air each year.

A New York waitress posts a new smoking sign in compliance with a 1988 city ordinance that strictly limits smoking in public places. Passive smoking, or inhaling another's smoke, can thus be minimized.

In 1987, in New Jersey alone, 60,000 factories were licensed to vent pollutants into the air. That same year, authorities in Texas estimated that about 1,000 different chemicals entered the air there every day; once airborne, they combined to form perhaps 10,000 chemical compounds, many of which are unknown and do not even have scientific names. Only 6 are federally regulated, and altogether about 62 million pounds of man-made pollutants now enter the air each year in the United States.

In 1976, in Seveso, Italy, one possible result of air pollution showed itself dramatically when a nearby factory exploded, forming a huge cloud of toxic gas over the town. The cloud held between 22 and 132 pounds of a chemical called dioxin, and forced the town's 730 inhabitants to flee their homes. (Dioxin is so toxic that three ounces could kill the population of New York City.) From Seveso, dioxin soaked into the water, the earth, and the animals, poisoning everything nearby for longer than anyone knows and spreading farther into the environment than anyone has yet been able to measure.

But undetectable traces of air pollutants may be even worse, because we do not know they are there, and their effects are felt only over a long time. As pollution researcher Michael Brown writes, "The problem is not so much thick smoke that causes odors and wheezing, but invisible gases and fine particles that can throw a wrench into the tiniest mechanisms of a cell." Such invisible damage may take 30 or 40 years to appear, or may show itself in a person's children through genetic damage and birth defects.

A source of pollution unsuspected until recently is radon gas. When the uranium ore often present in granite and some other rocks breaks down (it decomposes naturally), radon gas is produced. Houses built on soil that gives off radon gas may trap the gas so that high concentrations of it form in these houses. Ventilation fans may disperse it to safe levels, but because it is invisible and has no odor, people do not know if their houses are radon contaminated unless the houses are tested.

In 1984, one house tested in Pennsylvania had levels of radon-gas radioactivity 700 times higher than the maximum amount

In 1977, a ban on aerosol fluorocarbons was passed in Oregon. Fluorocarbons threaten the earth's ozone layer, which filters the sun's rays.

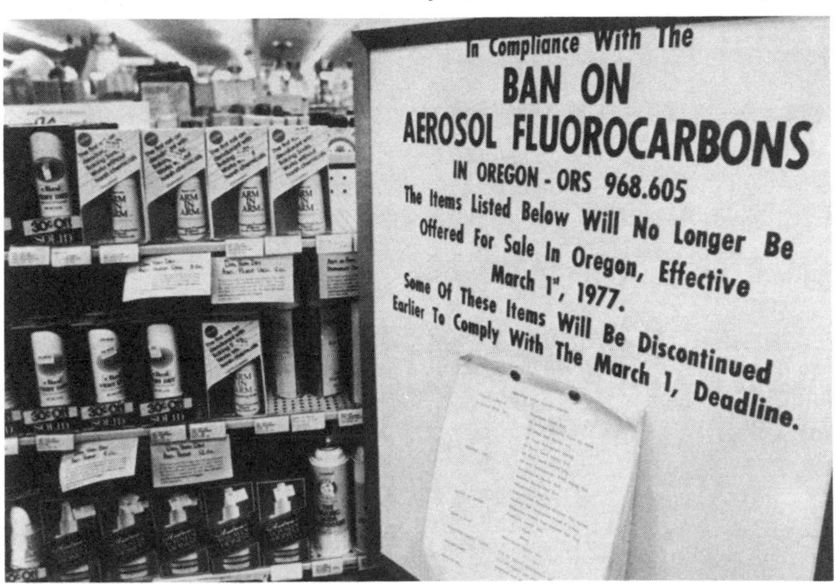

recommended for human exposure. This was discovered only because the homeowner worked at a nuclear plant and had to pass through radiation detectors that showed he was receiving radiation contamination at home. The EPA explained that living in that house was equivalent, in terms of the cancer risk it caused, to smoking 280 packs of cigarettes per day. Each year the homeowner and his family spent in the house raised each family member's cancer risk by 14%.

The house was decontaminated, its foundation dug up and sealed with plastic, and sophisticated ventilation fans installed at a total cost of about $32,000. It is now safe to live in—but the EPA does not know how many other houses are similarly contaminated, and neither do the people living in the houses.

In some areas, 60% of the houses tested have contained dangerous quantities of radon gas. The EPA estimates that 8 million houses or more in the United States may contain too much radon. In 1986, Congress appropriated $5 million to look for radon in houses across the nation, find ways to reduce it, and teach people

Residents of Seveso, Italy, return to their homes nearly four months after the 1976 factory explosion that released toxic gas into the air.

The Watras family in front of their Boyertown, Pennsylvania, home, one of the first in the nation known to be contaminated with radon gas. In some areas of the country, 60% of the houses are contaminated.

about it. In 1987, an EPA-sponsored national survey to learn more about the extent of radon contamination began. Early estimates say that it could cost more than $400 billion to clean up the nation's radon-contaminated homes.

Working for Cleaner Air

In order to reduce the number of threats to the respiratory system, a number of organizations both private and public are working for cleaner air. Private groups include the Sierra Club, the Air Pollution Control Association, the American Lung Association, the American Cancer Society, the American Public Health Association, and the American Association for Respiratory Therapy.

Government groups include federal, state, and local environmental protection agencies, the Council on Environmental Quality, the National Science Foundation, the Occupational Safety and Health Review Commission, the National Academy of Sciences, and the National Institutes of Health.

Because air moves freely all over the world, environmental threats to breathing are not only local or national problems but threats to healthy living everywhere. Canada, Australia, Japan, Brazil, and Mexico, as well as the nations of Europe, all have air-pollution problems and programs for reducing them: In Brazil, many motor vehicles run on gasohol, an alcohol/gasoline fuel made partly from sugarcane, which produces fewer toxic substances when burned, whereas Japanese factories are required to use the most modern pollution-reducing technology available. One international group working toward better breathing everywhere is the United Nations' World Health Organization. It studies respiratory health and disease, monitors air cleanliness, and reports problems, goals, and achievements in these matters around the world.

People of any age may help protect their own respiratory system by avoiding cigarettes and illicit drugs and alcohol, by taking good care of their general health to prevent infection, and by being aware of air pollution and avoiding it when they can. This involves taking safety precautions in dusty or fume-polluted areas and workplaces, and better yet, avoiding such places if possible.

• • • •

CHAPTER 8

ON THE HORIZON

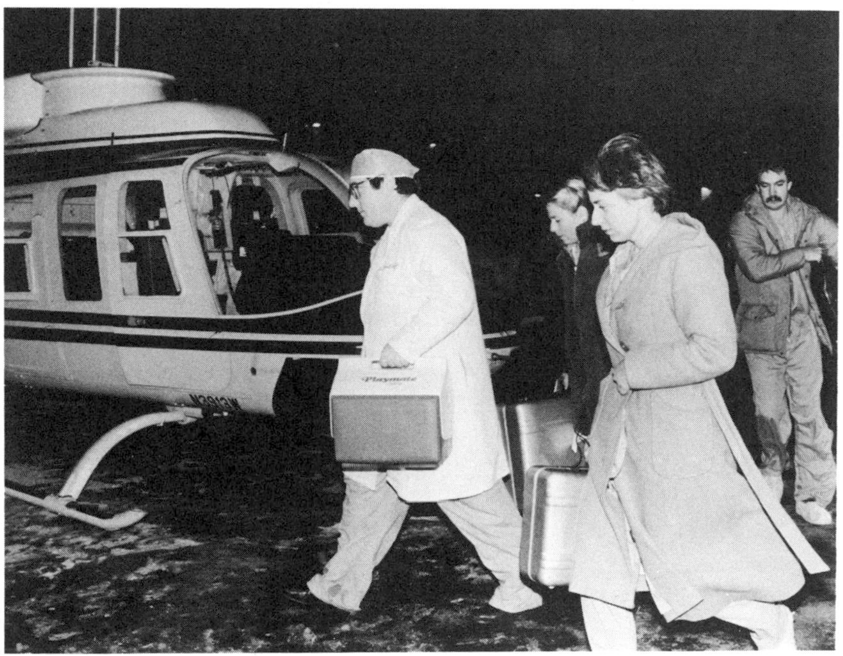
Transplant team with donated organ

Medical science has come a long way in understanding how the respiratory system works and what can be done when it malfunctions. One of the most dramatic demonstrations of this is in organ transplantation—the surgical replacement of body organs that fail to do their job because of disease, injury, or congenital malformation.

The lungs are among the most difficult of organs to transplant. Because their blood supply is so intimately connected with that of the heart, lungs are not often transplanted without also replacing the heart, in a combination heart/lung transplant operation.

To date, only about 250 such operations have been performed at 10 medical centers in the United States, but about 66% of the patients who have received new lungs and a heart have survived for at least a year, and 25% have lived more than 5 years.

In 1987, a dramatic "domino surgery" showed just how useful such transplants can be. At the University of Baltimore, the heart and lungs were removed from an accident victim whose brain had died but whose other organs continued functioning. At the same time, Clinton House, a 28-year-old mechanic, was having his own heart and lungs removed. His lungs were ruined by cystic fibrosis, but his heart was healthy; he was getting a new heart simply because it was the only way he could get the lungs he needed.

So while House received the heart and lungs of the accident victim, he donated his "old" heart, which was still perfectly useful, to John Couch, a 38-year-old man with advanced heart disease. Both House and Couch survived their surgery, but House died 14 months later of complications arising from organ rejection. The event marked the first time in the United States that a living individual had donated his heart, and it gave cystic fibrosis victims new hope for a life without the debilitating disease.

Cystic fibrosis is just one lung disease for which heart-lung transplants offer new hope. In England, one cystic fibrosis victim has survived 20 months after such surgery and is able to continue to work as a librarian. Although cystic fibrosis affects the whole body so that new lungs do not cure it entirely, the British patient's new lungs have not shown signs of being affected by the disease.

Primary pulmonary hypertension is another disease for which heart-lung transplantation has been done. It occurs when, for unknown reasons, the blood pressure in the respiratory system's blood vessels is too high. The high pressure eventually destroys the lungs. So far in the United States, about 50 heart-lung transplants have been performed to cure this disease; the 1-year survival rate is about 50%.

The transplanting of lungs alone is still in its early stages. But in Toronto, Dr. Joel Cooper of the Toronto General Hospital has done more than half a dozen such surgeries; two of his patients have survived since 1983. Several had emphysema, the "smoker's disease," and probably would have died within months without the surgery.

In the United States, "lungs alone" surgery is performed at only one medical center: Montefiore Medical Center in New York. Coupled with the technical problems of the procedure, the scarcity of donated organs makes lung transplantation a rare operation. But as technical expertise and public awareness of the benefits of organ donation grow, this type of surgery is likely to be done more often.

Of course it would be better if transplants were not necessary—if diseases such as emphysema and cystic fibrosis could be pre-

When cystic fibrosis victim Clinton House (right) received a heart-lung transplant, he donated his own heart to John Couch. Although House died 14 months later, he was the country's first living heart donor.

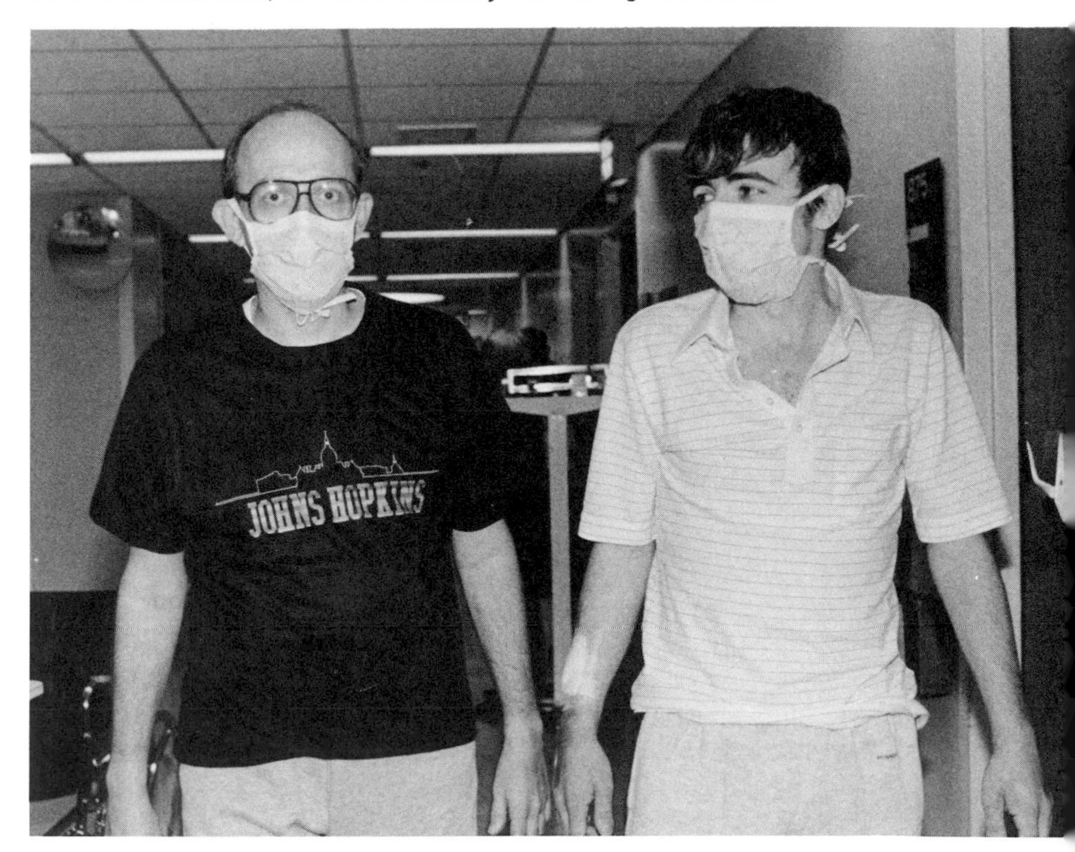

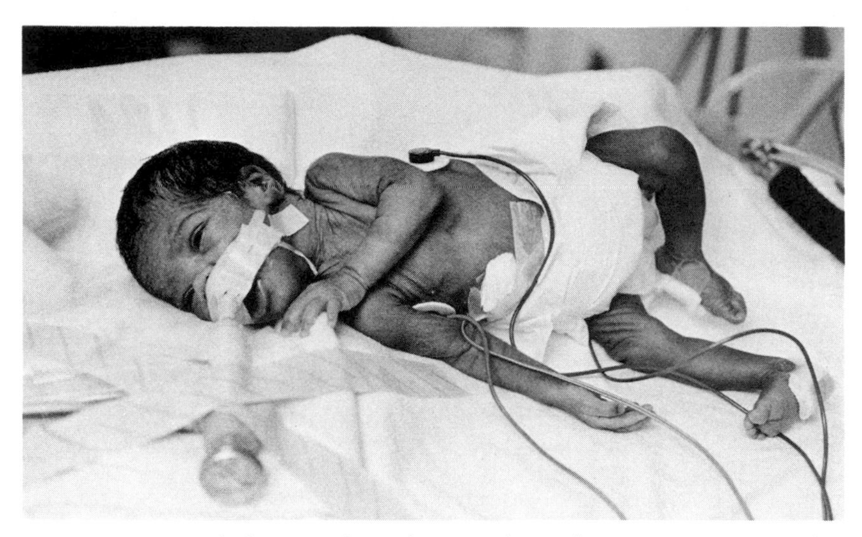

Many premature babies, such as the one shown here, are put on respirators until their lungs are fully formed.

vented. To try to prevent lung diseases caused by smoking, the American Cancer Society and the American Lung Association offer stop-smoking clinics and public information programs on the dangers of smoking, including a "Smoke-Free Young America by the Year 2000" initiative. Since 1976 the stop-smoking message seems to have been heard: The percentage of high-school seniors who smoke daily has decreased from 28.8 to 19.5%, and the number of adult male smokers has decreased from 42 to 32%.

The prevention of genetic lung diseases such as cystic fibrosis was advanced in 1987 when scientists at California's Integrated Genetics, Incorporated, found the genetic marker—the piece of the cell's inner machinery—that shows cystic fibrosis in a person's body before symptoms of the disease appear, and sometimes even before an infant is born. The next step in preventing the disease is "gene therapy"—changing the machinery in cells so that the cells function normally, stopping the disease before it has a chance to develop. As of yet, however, this has not become a reality.

Lung disease in premature infants (babies born before they are mature enough to live outside their mothers) affects about 50,000 infants in the United States each year. Because many such infants do not have enough surfactant in their lungs, their lungs collapse. Some can be kept alive on respirators until their lungs develop, but such treatments themselves cause different forms of lung disease and other problems as well.

By contrast, mature unborn infants' lungs make extra surfactant and excrete this substance into the amniotic fluid—the liquid that surrounds the infant in the mother's womb. In light of this, Dr. T. Allen Merritt, professor of pediatrics and neonatal medicine at the University Hospital of San Diego County, established an amniotic fluid bank in San Diego, California. There, amniotic fluid is donated by mothers who are about to give birth to mature babies and is given to babies whose lungs are not mature. Although studies of the procedure are not yet complete, the surfactant in the donated fluid seems to protect some infants from lung disease.

Two other groups of doctors, in Toronto, Canada, and in Rochester and Buffalo, New York, give surfactant from calves' lungs to premature babies. In one study, only 2 of 14 babies treated with the calf surfactant got lung disease, whereas half of 13 who did not receive the surfactant got the disease. Thus, the calf surfactant seems to have prevented the disease in infants who received it.

Damage to the lungs from infections might be prevented if the infections themselves were prevented. Such prevention is being advanced by research on the immune system—the body's own

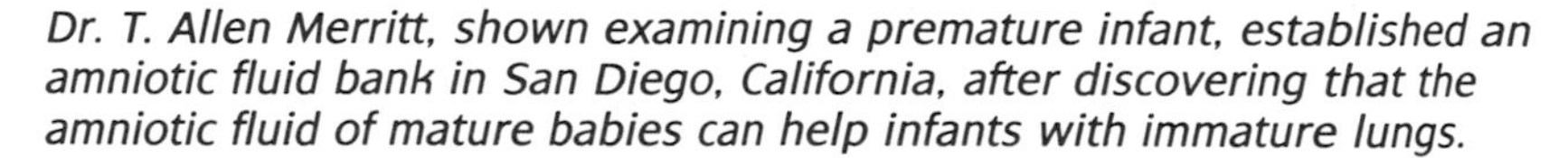

Dr. T. Allen Merritt, shown examining a premature infant, established an amniotic fluid bank in San Diego, California, after discovering that the amniotic fluid of mature babies can help infants with immature lungs.

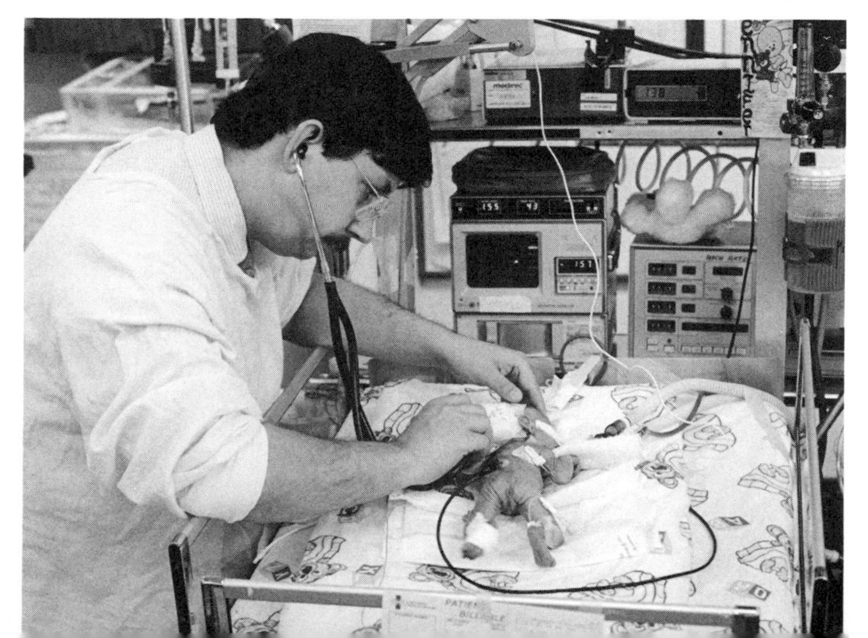

defense against infection. The immune system is not yet fully understood by medical science. But current research on it, fueled by the AIDS crisis (AIDS, or acquired immune deficiency syndrome, is a disease that disables the immune system) is proceeding daily at medical centers around the world.

Accidents that injure the neck or back can paralyze the respiratory system by severing the spinal cord, which sends messages from the brain to the major muscle of respiration, the diaphragm. Normally, breathing messages travel from the spinal cord to the diaphragm along the phrenic nerve. Recently, Dr. William Glenn developed a phrenic pacer, a device that delivers a small electrical signal through a wire to the phrenic nerve, triggering an artificial "breathe" signal to a paralyzed person's diaphragm. With the phrenic pacer, a person who would otherwise have to depend on a mechanical respirator—a "breathing machine"—can breathe independently.

The phrenic pacer has limitations: It does not respond to a person's "need" to breathe, but to a preset breathing rate. And it can only be used in a person whose general health (except for paralysis) is fairly good; severe infections, for example, limit its use. Also, it does not prevent many complications of paralysis that attack the respiratory system. Because a person using it cannot cough, for example, he or she is unusually susceptible to pneumonia. In the future, there is the hope of making phrenic pacers that respond to oxygen and carbon dioxide levels in the blood just as the brain normally does and that allow a person to trigger deep breaths and forceful exhalations for coughing purposes.

Transplants, genetic research, investigation of the immune system, and mechanical devices such as phrenic pacers are already helping thousands of people who suffer from breathing disabilities. But all of these therapies are only in their beginning stages, and the best treatment for most respiratory problems is still prevention.

By taking precautions and making the effort to avoid pollutants and damaging habits such as smoking and drug and alcohol use, young people today may protect their own lungs, those of their families and friends, and the breathing of the children they may someday wish to raise. They may, in fact, make a vital difference in the matter of life and breath for everyone.

• • • • • • •

FOR MORE INFORMATION

The following is a list of national and state organizations that can provide additional information regarding the respiratory system and respiratory disorders or recommend other agencies that can be of further assistance.

American Cancer Society
777 Third Avenue
New York, NY 10017
(For the office nearest you, consult your local telephone directory.)

American Lung Association, National Headquarters
1740 Broadway
New York, NY 10019
(212) 315-8700

Association for the Care of Asthma
c/o Herbert C. Mansmann, Jr., M.D.
Jefferson Medical College
1025 Walnut Street, Room 727
Philadelphia, PA 19107
(215) 928-8912

Asthma Care Association of America
Spring Valley Road
Ossining, NY 10562
(914) 762-1941

Asthmatic Children's Association of New York
Spring Valley Road
Ossining, NY 10562
(914) 762-1941

Congress of Lung Association Staff
1740 Broadway
New York, NY 10019
(212) 315-8802

Cystic Fibrosis Foundation
6931 Arlington Road, #200
Bethesda, MD 20814

The Cystic Fibrosis Organization
6000 Executive Boulevard, Suite 510
Rockville, MD 20852
(301) 881-9130
(800) FIGHT CF

Emphysema Anonymous, Inc.
P.O. Box 3224
Seminole, FL 33542
(813) 391-9977

Lung Hotline
(800) 222-LUNG
Colorado: (303) 398-1477

National Cancer Institute Hotline
(800) 638-6694

National Coalition of Black Lung and Respiratory Disease Clinics
c/o REACHS
P.O. Box 209
Main Street
Jacksboro, TN 37757
(615) 562-1156

National Foundation for Asthma
P.O. Box 30069
Tucson, AZ 85751
(602) 323-6056

National Heart, Lung, and Blood Institute
National Institutes of Health
9000 Rockville Pike
Building 31, 4A21
Bethesda, MD 20892
(301) 496-4236

National Institute of Allergy and Infectious Diseases NIAID/NIH
9000 Rockville Pike
Building 31, Room 7A32
Bethesda, MD 20892
(301) 496-5717

National Jewish Center for Immunology and Respiratory Medicine
1400 Jackson Street
Denver, CO 80206
(303) 388-4461

For information on legal and environmental issues pertaining to the respiratory system, contact the following:

American Academy of Environmental Sciences
P.O. Box 16106
Denver, CO 80216

American Institute of Medical Climatology
1023 Welsh Road
Philadelphia, PA 19115
(215) 673-8368

Environmental Protection Agency
401 M Street SW
Washington, DC 20460

Feingold Association of the United States
Drawer AG
Holtsville, NY 11742
(516) 543-4658

Human Ecology Action League
7330 N. Rogers Avenue
Chicago, IL 60626
(312) 665-6575

National Accreditation Council for Environmental Health Curricula
c/o Professor James Lucas
College of Science and Engineering
Wright State University
Dayton, OH 45431
(513) 873-2083

National Environmental Health Association
720 S. Colorado Boulevard, Suite 970, South Tower
Denver, CO 80222

Office of Safety and Health Administration
200 Constitution Avenue
Washington, DC 20210

Office of Science and Technology
Old Executive Office Building
Washington, DC 20506

Society for Environmental Geochemistry and Health
c/o Nord L. Gale
Life Science Department
University of Missouri
Rolla, MO 65401
(314) 341-4831

FURTHER READING

Berland, Theodore. *Living with Your Allergies and Asthma.* New York: St. Martin's Press, 1983.

Cherniak, Reuben M., M.D., Louis Cherniak, M.D., and Arnold Naimark, M.D. *Respiration in Health and Disease.* Philadelphia: Saunders, 1972.

Cumming, Gordon. *Disorders of the Respiratory System.* Oxford, England: Blackwell Scientific Publications, 1980.

DeKornfeld, Thomas J., M.D. *Anatomy and Physiology for Respiratory Therapy.* Sarasota, FL: Glenn Educational Medical Services, 1976.

Edwards, D. D. "Mending a Torn Lung: (Emphysema) Antitrypsin Therapy." *Science News* 131 (May 2, 1987): 277.

Haas, François. *The Essential Asthma Book.* New York: Scribners, 1987.

La Favore, Michael. *Radon: The Invisible Threat.* Emmaus, PA: Rodale Press, 1987.

Loomis, C. "Childhood Asthma: What You Should Know." *Parents* 62 (May 1987): 227.

Luce, John M. *Intensive Respiratory Care.* Philadelphia: Saunders, 1984.

Monastersky, R. "Lung Cancer Risks from Radon Exposure." *Science News* 133 (January 16, 1988): 39.

Petty, Thomas L., M.D., and Louise M. Nett. *Enjoying Life with Emphysema.* Philadelphia: Lee & Febiger, 1984.

Silverstein, Alvin. *Itch, Sniffle & Sneeze.* New York: Four Winds Press, 1978.

Slonim, N. Balfour, M.D., and Lyle H. Hamilton. *Respiratory Physiology.* St. Louis: C. V. Mosby, 1972.

Wallis, Claudia. "The Hearts of the Matter." *Time* 129 (May 25, 1987): 60.

Weibel, Ewald R. *The Pathway for Oxygen.* Cambridge, MA: Harvard University Press, 1984.

Weinstein, Allan, M.D. *Asthma.* New York: McGraw-Hill, 1987.

Young, Stuart H. *The Asthma Handbook: A Complete Guide for Patients and Their Families.* New York: Bantam, 1985.

PICTURE CREDITS

American Cancer Society Television Spot, "Dreams": p. 67; AP/Wide World Photos: pp. 79, 82, 87, 89; Art Resource: p. 43; The Bettmann Archive: pp. 15, 26, 57, 62, 68, 83, 84, 85; Bruce Coleman, Inc.: p. 29; March of Dimes Birth Defects Foundation: p. 91; Phiz Mezey: p. 90; New York Lung Association: p. 24; Alfred Pasieka/Taurus Photos: cover; Reuters/Bettmann: p. 73; Taurus Photos: pp. 13, 17, 30, 31, 32, 33, 35, 37, 49, 59, 64, 70, 71, 75, 80; UPI/Bettmann: pp. 15, 26, 57, 62, 68, 83, 84, 85; Original illustrations by Robert Margulies: pp. 39, 40, 41, 45, 51, 52, 60, 75.

GLOSSARY

acinus the berrylike ending of a tiny airway in the lung, where the aleveoli are located
alveolus a tiny air sac in the lung where oxygen is transferred from the lung to the blood
anatomy the structure of the body
aorta the main blood vessel from the heart to the body
aortic body a group of cells in the aorta that sense oxygen levels in the blood
arteriole a tiny artery, especially one that branches into a capillary
asbestos any of several minerals used in making insulation
asthma a disease in which breathing passages constrict, causing shortness of breath

bagassosis lung disease caused by inhaling sugarcane dust
bronchiole one of the lung's smallest air tubes
bronchitis inflammation of the lung's air tubes
bronchodilator medicine to relax constricted smooth muscle around the airways
bronchospasm tightening of breathing passages caused by spasm of smooth muscle around them
bronchus a large air tube in the lung
byssinosis lung disease caused by inhaling cotton fibers

capillary a tiny blood vessel
carbon dioxide the gas produced as a waste product by metabolism in cells
carotid body a group of cells in the carotid artery that senses oxygen levels in the blood
cartilage bonelike tissues in the body, but softer and more flexible than bone
cell the smallest building block in living material
cell wall the outer skin or membrane of a cell
chronic tending to continue over time

ciliated columnar epithelium skin with cilia and goblet cells that lines the respiratory system
cilium a hairlike structure projecting from the surface of a cell
circulatory system the system through which blood moves in the body; composed of the heart and blood vessels
congenital existing since birth
COLD chronic obstructive lung disease; disease resulting from chronic bronchitis and emphysema, in which the lungs can no longer fully perform their function of ventilation
cricoid cartilage one of the cartilages in the trachea, the body's main air tube
cystic fibrosis a disease that causes glands in the body to secrete thick mucus

dehydration loss or deficiency of water in body tissues
diaphragm the body's main breathing muscle
diffusion movement across a membrane from an area where a substance is more concentrated to one where it is less concentrated

epiglottis the flap that acts as a lid on the larynx
exhale breathe out
exocrine denoting a gland that secretes outwardly through a duct
extrinsic from outside

farmer's lung lung disease caused by inhaling fibers from moldy hay

gill structure through which water-dwelling animals extract oxygen from water
glottis part of the larynx containing the vocal cords
goblet cell cells that produce mucus in the lung

hemoglobin substance in the red blood cells that binds with oxygen to transport it
hilus entry point in the lung for vessels, nerves, and bronchi

inhale breathe in
intercostal muscles muscles between the ribs that aid in breathing
intrinsic from inside
invertebrate without a spine

kidney organ that removes liquid waste from the body

lamellae thin sheets in a gill that add surface area so more water can flow over it

laryngospasm spasmodic closure of the muscles of the larynx
larynx the upper part of the respiratory system between the pharynx and trachea, where the vocal cords are located
lobe a projection or division of any organ, especially of the brain, lungs, and glands
lung the main breathing organ of the body

macrophage cell that captures and digests foreign bacteria
mediastinum middle portion of the chest, where the heart and esophagus are located
metabolism chemical processes by which food is turned into energy the body can use
metamorphosis change in shape, as in the change from caterpillar to butterfly or tadpole to frog
micron a thousandth of a millimeter
millimeter one thousandth of a meter; one inch equals 2 1/2 millimeters
molecule the smallest possible quantity of a substance made of one or more atoms

nasopharynx the upper portion of the respiratory system, near the palate

operculum the cover over a fish's gill
oropharynx the upper portion of the respiratory system, near the mouth
osmosis process of diffusion through a membrane
oxygen gas used by the body's cells in metabolism
oxyhemoglobin molecule made when oxygen and hemoglobin combine in a red blood cell; the form in which oxygen is transported from lungs to tissues where oxygen is released

percussion tapping on the chest to determine presence of fluid in the lungs
permeable having pores or membranes that permit liquids or gases to pass through
pharynx the inner mouth area below the nasal cavities and above the larynx
phrenic nerve nerve connecting spinal cord to diaphragm
physiology the way the body works
plasma clear fluid remaining when cells are filtered from blood
pleura slippery covering inside chest and over lungs
pneumonia viral or bacterial infection of lung leading to inflammation
pneumothorax hole in the lung causing it to collapse
pranayama Hindu breathing control technique
prognosis likely outcome of a disease

protozoan a primitive one-celled organism
pulmonary having to do with the lungs
pulmonary circulation blood vessels from the heart to the lungs

radon gas produced when radioactive material such as uranium disintegrates
red blood cell cell in blood that caries oxygen to body cells
residual volume air that remains in lungs after a person breathes out as much as possible
respiration movement of oxygen from atmosphere to cells and carbon dioxide from cells to atmosphere
respiratory centers areas in the brain that sense carbon dioxide levels in blood and stimulate breathing
respiratory system the body system that delivers oxygen to body and removes waste carbon dioxide

scalene muscles muscles between neck and upper ribs that assist in breathing
siderosis lung disease caused by inhaling iron dust
silicosis lung disease caused by inhaling dust from the mineral silicon
sternum flat bone at the middle of the chest
stethoscope instrument for hearing air movement in the lungs
surface tension condition resulting from forces that cause liquids to form flat surfaces
surfactant substance produced by lungs to lower surface tension in alveoli; its bubbles hold lungs open
systemic circulation movement of blood from the heart to all parts of the body but the lungs

thyroid cartilage one of the cartilages in the trachea
trachea the body's main air tube

umbilical cord the connecting cord between a mother and her unborn infant through which the mother's body nourishes the infant

vertebrate having a spine
virus very tiny disease-causing organism
vocal cords tissues in the larynx through which air is forced to make sounds

INDEX

Mary Kittredge, a former associate editor of the medical journal *Respiratory Care,* is a free-lance writer of nonfiction and fiction. She is certified as a respiratory-care technician by the American Association for Respiratory Therapy and has been a member of the respiratory-care staff at Yale–New Haven Hospital and Medical Center since 1972.

Ms. Kittredge was educated at Trinity College, Hartford, and the University of California Medical Center, San Francisco. She is the author of *Organ Transplants* and *Prescription & Over-the-Counter Drugs* in the Chelsea House ENCYCLOPEDIA OF HEALTH series, and of young-adult biographies *Marc Antony, Frederick the Great,* and *Jane Addams.* Her writing awards include the Ruell Crompton Tuttle Essay Prize and the Mystery Writers of America Robert L. Fish Award for best first short-mystery fiction of 1986.

Dale C. Garell, M.D., is medical director of California Childrens Services, Department of Health Services, County of Los Angeles. He is also clinical professor in the Department of Pediatrics and Family Medicine at the University of Southern California School of Medicine and Visiting associate clinical professor of maternal and child health at the University of Hawaii School of Public Health. From 1963 to 1974, he was medical director of the Division of Adolescent Medicine at Children's Hospital in Los Angeles. Dr. Garell has served as president of the Society for Adolescent Medicine, chairman of the youth committee of the American Academy of Pediatrics, and as a forum member of the White House Conference on Children (1970) and White House Conference on Youth (1971). He has also been a member of the editorial board of the *American Journal of Diseases of Children.*

C. Everett Koop, M.D., Sc.D., is Surgeon General, Deputy Assistant Secretary for Health, and Director of the Office of International Health of the U.S. Public Health Service. A pediatric surgeon with an international reputation, he was previously surgeon-in-chief of Children's Hospital of Philadelphia and professor of pediatric surgery and pediatrics at the University of Pennsylvania. Dr. Koop is the author of more than 175 articles and books on the practice of medicine. He has served as surgery editor of the *Journal of Clinical Pediatrics* and editor-in-chief of the *Journal of Pediatric Surgery.* Dr. Koop has received nine honorary degrees and numerous other awards, including the Denis Brown Gold Medal of the British Association of Paediatric Surgeons, the William E. Ladd Gold Medal of the American Academy of Pediatrics, and the Copernicus Medal of the Surgical Society of Poland. He is a Chevalier of the French Legion of Honor and a member of the Royal College of Surgeons, London.